DEADLY
VOYAGE

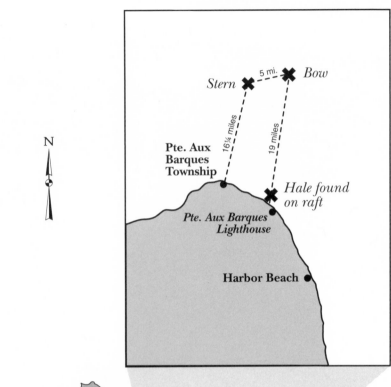

Stern · 5 mi. · Bow

16¼ miles

19 miles

**Pte. Aux
Barques
Township**

*Hale found
on raft*

*Pte. Aux Barques
Lighthouse*

Harbor Beach ●

N

Saginaw ●

Port Huron ●

Detroit ●

DEADLY VOYAGE

THE S.S. *DANIEL J. MORRELL* TRAGEDY

ANDREW KANTAR

MICHIGAN STATE UNIVERSITY PRESS · EAST LANSING

⊖ The paper used in this publication meets the minimum requirements of ANSI/
NISO Z39.48-1992 (R 1997) (Permanence of Paper).

 Michigan State University Press
East Lansing, Michigan 48823-5245

Printed and bound in the United States of America.

15 14 13 12 11 10 09   1 2 3 4 5 6 7 8 9 10

LIBRARY OF CONGRESS CATALOGING-IN-PUBLICATION DATA
Kantar, Andrew Klekner.
Deadly voyage : the S.S. Daniel J. Morrell tragedy / Andrew Kantar.
p. cm.
Includes bibliographical references.
ISBN 978-0-87013-863-8 (paper : alk. paper) 1. Daniel J. Morrell (Ship) 2. Shipwrecks—
Huron, Lake (Mich. and Ont.) 3. Hale, Dennis. 4. Shipwreck victims—Huron, Lake (Mich.
and Ont.)—Biography. 5. Survival after airplane accidents, shipwrecks, etc.—Huron, Lake
(Mich. and Ont.) 6. Huron, Lake (Mich. and Ont.)—History—20th century. I. Title.
G530.D252K367 2009
917.7404—dc22
2009001320

Cover and book design by Charlie Sharp, Sharp Des!gns, Lansing, Michigan
Cover photograph of the S.S. *Daniel J. Morrell* was taken by Emory Massman just days
before it sank, and is used with permission of the photographer.

g green Michigan State University Press is a member of the Green Press Initiative
press and is committed to developing and encouraging ecologically responsible
INITIATIVE
publishing practices. For more information about the Green Press Initiative and the use
of recycled paper in book publishing, please visit *www.greenpressinitiative.org*.

Visit Michigan State University Press on the World Wide Web at *www.msupress.msu.edu*

For Ned and John,
my brothers and best friends

CONTENTS

ACKNOWLEDGMENTS

I am grateful to those who have contributed their time, resources, and support to this project. To begin, I wish to thank the following Michigan librarians and libraries for sharing their archival collections and reference resources: David Smith and Barbara King, St. Clair County Public Library (Port Huron); Mary McIntyre, Bad Axe Public Library; Alice and Jack Wirt Public Library (Bay City); Harbor Beach Public Library; and Big Rapids Public Library. Thanks are also due to those who provided the historical photographs that are reprinted in this book: Dennis Hale; Sandy Cleary Peer; Emory Massman; Robert W. Graham, archivist, Historical Collections of the Great Lakes, Bowling Green State University; Marianne Weldon, curator of collections, Detroit Historical Society and Dossin Great Lakes Museum; Jack Deo, Superior View Historic Photography and Art Gallery Photographs; Port Huron *Times Herald*, and Valley Camp Ship Museum (Sault Ste. Marie).

Special acknowledgment is due to Sandy Cleary Peer and Joe Stojek, both of whom generously shared recollections of their loved ones. I also wish to thank maritime author Mike Schumacher for generously agreeing to read the manuscript. I am particularly grateful to the *Morrell*'s only survivor, Dennis Hale, for meeting with me, sharing his thoughtful insights, and his willingness to read and comment on this manuscript. In addition, his book, *Sole Survivor: Dennis Hale's Own Story*, proved an invaluable resource as the only eyewitness account of the *Morrell* tragedy.

Special thanks to Julie Loehr and Martha Bates of Michigan State University Press for believing in my work and for their continued support during the many years we have worked together. I also sincerely appreciate the hard work of Kristine Blakeslee, Annette Tanner, and Julie Reaume of MSU Press.

I gratefully acknowledge the memory of my parents, Bruce and Sally, for their loving guidance and for teaching me a lifelong respect for learning. Heartfelt thanks to our children, Sally, Max, and Emily, for their support and encouragement. Deepest gratitude goes to my wife, Fran, whose impeccable judgment and unwavering patience are my rock.

CHAPTER ONE

THE GREAT NOVEMBER TERROR

I magine a lake so vast that you cannot even see the other side. The seemingly endless expanse reaches all the way to a watery horizon, where it is joined by the infinite sky. Now, imagine five of these magnificent bodies of water, all connected, whose basins were gouged out of the earth thousands of years ago by crawling glaciers and then filled with the remnants of their melted bodies—water. These are the Great Lakes—indeed a remarkable geologic creation, left to us from the Pleistocene epoch of the Ice Age about 11,000 years ago. Together they stretch east to west, New York to Minnesota, for more than a thousand miles and represent the world's largest supply of fresh water. They are Lakes Ontario, Erie, Huron, Michigan, and Superior—the Great Lakes.

As awe-inspiring as they are to see, photograph, and paint, as enjoyable as they are to swim in and sail on, these lakes have served another important purpose. For centuries they have served as the trade routes for people who needed to travel great distances or haul heavy loads across the Midwest. From the canoes of Indians and the French Canadian voyageurs to the massive 1,000-foot freighters of today, the lakes have connected cultures, countries, and cities. In fact, it is no coincidence that some of North America's most powerful industrial centers, like Chicago, Detroit,

Toronto, and Cleveland, developed on the shores of these lakes. Today, the main freight is iron ore, used in the making of steel, but grain is also a major cargo for these mighty steamships.

Because of their massive size and the sudden storms that changing weather can generate, the Great Lakes have been responsible for some of the most disastrous shipwrecks in history. Though no one knows for sure how many ships the lakes have claimed, by some estimates there have been more than 6,000 shipwrecks, and 35,000 lives have been lost. Gale-force winds that can reach sixty to seventy miles per hour and waves that top a staggering thirty-five feet make the violent moods of the Great Lakes some of the most intimidating and dangerous forces in nature. Only the foolhardy ignore how treacherous these natural giants become when bad weather blows across them. With astonishing power, they can take a ship the length of two football fields and unmercifully twist her until she rips in half!

And at no time are the lakes more unpredictable and dangerous than in the stormy month of November. The contorted wrecks that rest on the muddy bottoms of all of the lakes speak silently to the countless horrors of vicious storms that have claimed the lives of thousands of ill-fated sailors, leaving behind their mourning mothers, widowed wives, and fatherless children. Written in the lakes' mysterious depths are haunting tales, revealing an unleashed wrath. The lost ships buried in the murky waters across a thousand miles are carcasses of splintered timbers and twisted steel, each a silent grave, testament to a futile struggle. Most of these wrecks are long forgotten, but the stories of others are still told. One cold and stormy night on November 18, 1958, Lake Michigan claimed the giant steamer *Carl D. Bradley*, more than six hundred feet long. She was on her last voyage of the season, returning to port in Rogers City, the tiny Michigan town that most of the crew called home. Suddenly, in the midst of a brutal storm, a huge thud resounded through the ship. In the pilothouse, Captain Roland Bryan and First Mate Elmer Fleming spun around and looked down the length of the *Bradley*'s hull. They could not believe their eyes. The middle of the ship was bending, humping upward several feet in the air, lifted by the huge waves underneath.

Within minutes, before the eyes of her horrified crew, a raging sea tore the *Bradley* into two gigantic pieces.

Thirty-three men would die, while two others, Fleming and Deckwatch-man Frank Mays, would survive a fifteen-hour ordeal on a storm-tossed life raft in Lake Michigan. That night, twenty-three women were widowed, and fifty-three children lost their fathers. To this day, the *Carl D. Bradley* is the largest ship on the bottom of Lake Michigan.

In 1975, almost two decades after the *Bradley* was lost, on one hellish night in November, the most famous shipwreck in Great Lakes history took place. The freighter *Edmund Fitzgerald,* at over seven hundred feet long, became Lake Superior's largest and perhaps most mysterious victim. The *Fitz,* as she was called, was the pride of her fleet, breaking and setting shipping records and weathering mammoth storms during her seventeen-year lifetime. On that terrible night, immortalized in song and literature, the *Fitzgerald* and her crew of twenty-nine men fought bravely against a storm that spawned waves three stories high and hurricane-strength wind gusts of ninety-five miles per hour. The *Arthur Anderson,* another freighter, followed the *Fitzgerald,* tracking her on radar and maintaining radio contact with the *Fitzgerald*'s captain, Ernest McSorley. Captain Bernie Cooper of the *Anderson* knew that the *Fitzgerald* was taking on large amounts of water and was in serious trouble. Watching the *Fitzgerald* on his radar, Cooper feared that the big ship had bottomed out while navigating a perilous stretch called Six-Fathom Shoal, possibly tearing open her hull.

During the height of the storm, the *Fitzgerald* lost her radar and was sailing blindly into the unknown. The snow was blowing, the wind scream-ing, and the waves washing across the deck of the struggling freighter. Then in an instant Cooper saw the *Fitzgerald* drop from the radar screen, without even an SOS. Frantically, he attempted to make radio contact; the *Anderson* heard nothing but dead air. It was terrifying and mysterious. A ship of this size could not just drop from sight in an instant. Or could she?

Sadly, when the *Fitzgerald* lost her struggle with Superior, she was just seventeen miles from safe harbor at Whitefish Point, Michigan.

For decades, experts have debated the fate of the *Fitzgerald* in books, articles, and the news media, arguing different evidence to support their positions. There is no disagreement about why the *Fitzgerald* sank. Simply put, she took on too much water to remain buoyant. But why did she take on so much water?

Some say Captain Cooper was right, that the *Fitzgerald* scraped bottom (called shoaling) and damaged her hull on the pointed rocks of Six-Fathom Shoal. If a hole had been ripped in the bottom, water could have entered, causing the instability that led to her unexpected and tragic nosedive.

After an investigation, the Coast Guard concluded that the *Fitzgerald's* hatch cover clamps were loose, allowing water to enter the hold. All we know for sure are McSorley's own words that they were taking on water and had the pumps working. However, the water was pouring in faster than the pumps could work, and he could not stem the flow. But did this water come in from above through leaking hatch covers, or from below through a tear in the hull caused by shoaling?

Finally, there are those who subscribe to a big-wave theory. Captain Cooper considered this to be another possible cause. He recalled two thirty-five-foot waves exploding on the *Anderson* in rapid succession. Feeling fortunate to survive what could have been a deadly encounter, Cooper realized that the two rogue waves were rolling on a collision path with the *Fitzgerald* which was already struggling with a starboard list (leaning right). The monster waves would reach the *Fitzgerald* in just minutes. When the imperiled ship dropped from his radar, Cooper wondered if the *Fitzgerald* had taken the big seas across her bow, plunging nose down and propelling her five hundred feet to Superior's muddy bottom, where the wreck now rests in two pieces.

Perhaps a combination of these factors conspired against the doomed ship. Despite exhaustive research and the many theories offered, the *Fitzgerald's* sinking still remains a mystery.

■ CHAPTER TWO

THE SWEETWATER SEA

ong before French explorers of the early seventeenth century discovered the Great Lakes, Indians lived and traded on their shores. Tribes like the Ojibwa, Ottawa, Huron, Algonquin, Iroquois, and Erie hunted, fished, and farmed the lands and used the lakes for their trade routes. Probably the first white explorer to encounter the Great Lakes was Samuel de Champlain, who was searching for a Northwest Passage that would connect the Atlantic and Pacific. In 1603, the year of his first trip to North America, Champlain joined a fur-trading expedition and created a map of the St. Lawrence River. He published a report on New France, a region France had claimed in North America. Upon reading Champlain's account, King Henry IV asked him to serve as geographer for another expedition to New France and write about what he saw. Champlain believed that these inland seas would serve as a northern passage to the Pacific and ultimately as a trade route to China.

One intriguing member of Champlain's expedition was Étienne Brûlé. He was there when Champlain founded Quebec in 1608, and two years later Champlain asked him to live among the Huron Indians and learn from them. At that time, between 20,000 and 30,000 Huron lived in the region now known as Quebec. For several years, Brûlé lived with and respected the Huron people and their traditions. He is probably the first white explorer to see Lake Huron, or as the French called it, *La Mer Douce*—the Sweetwater Sea.

Fascinated by the Huron culture and a quick learner, Brûlé became so proficient with the language of the Huron tribe that he was Champlain's interpreter during his exploration of Lakes Huron and Ontario in 1615. Champlain and his men spent the winter in the land of the Huron, where he kept journals about their way of life. As an explorer and knowing there were waterways beyond Lake Huron, Champlain longed to go farther west in search of the Northwest Passage. But this was not to be, for beyond this great water were tribes with whom the Huron were at war. The Huron feared that the French would become the friends of their enemies. Champlain, therefore, remained with the Huron, chronicling their beliefs and culture. In 1616, Champlain's interpreter, Brûlé, was captured and tortured by the Iroquois, but he was eventually freed when he bluffed them into believing he would negotiate on their behalf with their enemies. Later, suspected of treachery, Brûlé would be killed by the Huron.

Bordering the province of Ontario and the state of Michigan, Lake Huron is second in size only to Lake Superior, the world's largest body of fresh water in surface area. Although Lakes Superior and Michigan are deeper, Huron's deepest spot is almost 750 feet, and it has an average depth of nearly 200 feet. Lake Huron is 206 miles long and 183 miles wide.

Sprawling Lake Huron includes two massive bays, Michigan's Saginaw Bay and Ontario's Georgian Bay. At almost two hundred miles long, Georgian Bay is about the same size as Lake Ontario! Including its 30,000 islands (mostly in Canada), Lake Huron has the Great Lakes' longest shoreline, winding just over 3,800 miles. In fact, separating Georgian Bay from the rest of Lake Huron is Manitoulin Island, the world's largest freshwater island. Manitoulin is so big it has 108 of its own lakes, including Lake Manitoulin, which is forty square miles. Manitoulin also has eighteen towns and 12,600 permanent residents.

Because Huron is an excellent transportation connection between Lake Erie and the western Great Lakes of Michigan and Superior, it is heavily traveled by the giant freighters. From ports in Lake Superior, such as Duluth, eastbound vessels with a load of iron ore go through Sault Ste. Marie and the locks of the St. Mary's River to gain access to Lake Huron and eventually down the St. Clair River to Lake Erie and ports like Cleveland or Buffalo. Or the steamers can follow the Straits of Mackinac into Lake Michigan and down to Chicago.

All of this shipping comes with a price, however. Because of its heavy shipping traffic, Huron may be responsible for more shipwrecks than any of the other lakes, laying claim to as many as 40 percent of all Great Lakes shipwrecks. Of these many shipwrecks, the *Daniel J. Morrell* is the largest to succumb to the depths of mighty Lake Huron. This reputation has made Lake Huron a force to be reckoned with and one that old salts do not take lightly, especially those sailors who have seen its darker side—and lived to tell the tale.

■ CHAPTER THREE

DEATH ON HURON

ach of the Great Lakes has its own tragic history, and Lake Huron's violent moods have become legendary. In fact, the first documented wreck on the lakes, the *Griffon,* went down on Lake Huron in 1679. About sixty years after Champlain's exploration of the lakes, the wealthy French explorer René-Robert Cavalier de La Salle built and sailed the *Griffon,* a handsome sixty-foot craft named after a mythical creature that was half lion and half eagle. Her outbound voyage to pick up valuable beaver pelts was not an easy one. Lake Erie tossed the little ship around, followed by some very rough sailing up Lake Huron, through the Straits of Mackinac, all the way over to Green Bay on Lake Michigan.

Loaded with a cargo of pelts, the *Griffon* planned to retrace her route across northern Lake Michigan, back through the Straits of Mackinac, and then down Lake Huron. LaSalle was not on board when, on her return trip, the little boat encountered a terrible September storm on Lake Huron. The four-day blow claimed the *Griffon* and her crew. Disappearing without a trace, the *Griffon* became the first known casualty of the Great Lakes.

Over the centuries, Lake Huron has been the site of thousands of shipwrecks. One of the most tragic events took place on the windy night of September 13, 1882. The steamer *Asia* was attempting to cross Georgian

Bay, filled to capacity with 125 passengers. In terrible, blowing seas, the ship sank at about eleven-thirty in the morning, but not before three lifeboats, filled with hopeful passengers, were launched. Only one of the lifeboats survived those wild seas. Several times they were overturned, and each time fewer people returned from the churning waters. Tossed around the great bay like a feather in the wind, the only remaining lifeboat was oarless and vulnerable on the open water. She eventually lost all but two of her passengers, seventeen-year-old Duncan Tinkiss and a young woman named Christina Ann Morrison, the cousin of the *Asia*'s first mate. The two nearly died, enduring two full days on the lake before their rescue. For the *Asia*'s other 123 passengers, there were no survival miracles. They were the silent victims of Georgian Bay's worst storm.

The "Great Storm of 1913," beginning with warnings on Friday, November 7, marked one of the most brutal weeks in the history of the Great Lakes. During the three-day siege, the lakes, especially Lake Huron, were relentlessly battered. It was a storm like no sailor had ever seen. Wreckage and debris from destroyed ships piled up six feet high along Huron's shoreline. Eight lakers, some over 500 feet long, were lost on Lake Huron. It didn't matter if the ships had years of service, like the Scottish-built *Wexford,* a sturdy Canadian freighter, or were brand-new, like the *James C. Carruthers*, on only her third trip. At 550 feet, the *Carruthers* was Canada's largest freighter. Both the *Wexford* and the *Carruthers* were lost with all hands. The same horrific fate was met by many other ships as the storm continued on its path of destruction. Among those on Lake Huron and in its path were the *Argus, Hydrus, Regina, John A. McGean,* and *Isaac M. Scott.* All were lost along with the life of every man on board. The human tragedy was monumental.

The *Charles S. Price,* a new 524-foot freighter carrying 9,000 tons of coal bound for Milwaukee, was another victim of the Great Storm. She was sailing without one of her crew, Milton Smith, the assistant engineer, who had a bad feeling about the weather forecast and decided to disembark while at the loading dock in Ashtabula, Ohio. Smith's feeling was right on target, for the *Price*'s journey was cut short when she came to a strange and tragic end.

It was a little before noon on Sunday, November 9, and the *Price* was close to Harbor Beach, on the northeast part of Michigan's "Thumb." Captain Bill Black sensed that the storm was starting to build on Lake Huron. The winds were gusting above forty miles per hour and the seas were worsening. Because of the threatening storm, the *Price* must have reversed her course in an effort to head back along the eastern shore of the Thumb and down to Port Huron.

The next morning, a freighter was observed completely upside down, about eight miles north of the St. Clair River. At the site, winds were blowing at seventy miles per hour, waves were cresting at forty feet, and a blizzard raged. Because of her unusual position, no one could read the name of what came to be known as the "mystery ship." The families of missing crew members in the Lake Huron region were tormented by the uncertainty of not knowing which vessel she was. Was she the ship that had carried their loved ones? Finally, five days later, the weather calmed enough for a diver to investigate the name on the submerged hull. She was the *Charles S. Price*. The entire crew of twenty-eight was lost. Some bodies washed ashore, but most remained in the doomed ship. Two days after her identity was revealed, the *Price* quietly slipped to the bottom of Lake Huron. For the families of the dead crew, uncertainty was replaced with unbearable grief.

The Great Storm's violence was unlike any other, not only because of its gusts of ninety miles per hour and forty-foot waves, but also because of its unusual duration. According to a 1913 report filed by the Lake Carriers' Association, storms of this strength and magnitude usually last four or five hours, but Lake Huron's deafening winds blew relentlessly at these frightening speeds for sixteen continuous hours! To make things even more treacherous, the wind would often blow one way and the sea amazingly would pull the other way, creating a cyclone-like effect. All of this, combined with blizzard snows, made the lake nearly impossible to navigate.

For days the furious winds and pelting snow continued. The nightmare would not end. At times, it seemed like the storm was weakening and then, just as suddenly, it blew itself into a frenzied terror. Through it all, icy bodies kept washing ashore. Men were found frozen in a grisly embrace or clinging futilely to life preservers with the name of a lost ship. Heartbreaking stories were told of bodies found on shore—frozen into one solid mass of humanity.

Amid the immeasurable wreckage of human suffering, the twisted steel and broken timbers of once-proud ships, and the tons of lost cargo, there were many inspiring tales of rescue and heroism. One of these involved the steamer *Howard M. Hanna, Jr.*, a 480-foot freighter hauling coal that was struggling mightily up Michigan's Huron coast, on her way to Lake Michigan and down to Milwaukee. Although her engines were going full steam, the powerful ship was practically at a standstill in the teeth of the great November blast. The winds and sea, gusting to seventy miles per hour, were so fierce that they exploded the windows in the pilothouse, drenching Captain William Hagan and two of his wheelsmen. By six-thirty in the evening, the engine room itself was under attack. Doors were smashed down and windows blown out, leaving the engineers in four feet of ice water. Next, the aft deckhouse or "boilerhouse," which included cabins and the ship's galley or "mess hall," totally collapsed, leaving food, broken china, silverware, and boxes to float in the now-flooded compartment.

The *Hanna* was showing severe damage, the effects of hours of savage pounding. To make matters even worse, at around eight o'clock at night she found herself caught in the trough of two waves, unable to right herself back out to sea. Though she put up a valiant struggle, with her propeller spinning helplessly out of the water, the *Hanna* was trapped, her deck awash with giant waves that unmercifully crashed upon it. By ten o'clock Lake Huron had its way, driving the hapless vessel onto the rocky reef off of the Port Austin Lighthouse, on the northern tip of Michigan's Thumb. Half of the crew huddled in the stern and the other half in the bow. They remained there all night, in the pitch dark, the sea pummeling the ship and flooding her deck.

In deep water and amid the never-ending pounding of the waves, the terrified crew of thirty-three, including one woman, felt their ship sinking. After receiving a distress signal from the imperiled ship, the men of the Pointe Aux Barques Lifesaving Station responded without delay. Courageously, the rescue team ventured out, inching their boat along against the freezing winds and deadly currents. But the sea dragged them back, dumping their boat on shore and weighing her down with heavy, wet sand.

The rescuers knew that under these extraordinary conditions, they might not be able to reach the *Hanna*'s helpless crew in time. They called for assistance from other lifesaving stations in the area. Unfortunately, they were busy helping other wrecked vessels and their crews. Consequently, the men of Pointe Aux Barques started to dig the sand out from their grounded boat. They did it with shovels, by hand, and in the drenching, icy winds. They had no choice; there was nothing else they could do. With each shovelful, the lake deposited another heavy load of sand on the boat they were desperately trying to free from the shore.

Soaked to the skin and physically done in, the men thought that at last they were ready to attempt another launch. However, their efforts met with more delays when they discovered their lifeboat had sustained at least five cracks and her wooden bottom had been punctured in several places after the heavy surf repeatedly tossed the boat back onto the beach. They made quick repairs, but by the time they finished, nightfall had made it impossible to venture out. The embattled crew of the *Hanna* prepared for a miserable night trapped on the deadly reef. Throughout the whole ordeal, the one woman aboard, Sadie Black, the second cook and wife of the steward, heroically prepared meals from whatever she could scare up in the flooded galley, while struggling waist deep through ice water!

Early the next morning, the rescuers made another attempt to send their small craft out in the direction of the *Hanna*. At the same time nine members of the *Hanna*'s crew made their own attempts to safety, rowing to shore in one of her lifeboats. The two boats passed each other. The *Hanna*'s lifeboat was headed for shore as the men from the lifesaving station continued in their badly patched lifeboat to rescue the remaining crew.

What a welcome sight the rescuers must have been to those who remained on the doomed *Hanna*. But the drama didn't end there. The repairs made on shore were no longer holding, and the lifeboat started filling with water! Desperately they bailed water as the *Hanna*'s exhausted crew climbed to what they hoped was safety.

In the end, the captain and entire crew of the *Hanna* were saved. Sadie Black, the brave woman who fed the men and helped care for their injuries, suffered from hypothermia but survived. To be sure, they were all hungry, cold, and exhausted, but most importantly, they were thankful to be alive, forever grateful to the fiercely determined men who never gave up on them.

The Great Storm caused $5 million in damaged or lost ships and cargo, roughly translating into at least $100 million today. As many as forty ships were wrecked, and thirty more suffered severe damage. As devastating as this carnage was to Great Lakes shipping, it could not compare to the pain of the families who lost loved ones. Despite the heroic and selfless efforts of many, a staggering 248 sailors drowned in the "White Hurricane," as it came to be known. On Lake Huron alone, eight freighters were lost and an astonishing 199 sailors perished!

A half century after the Great Storm and during the same dangerous month of November, the Sweetwater Sea was ravaged by another vicious storm that lasted for days. The year was 1966, eight years after the *Bradley* broke apart and less than a decade before the *Fitzgerald* plunged to her horrific end. It was the death storm of the *Daniel J. Morrell*. On November 29, twenty-eight men lost their lives to a sea so powerful that it ripped a six-hundred-foot giant in two. But unlike the eight freighters that were lost on Lake Huron with all hands, the *Morrell* had one crew member who miraculously survived. His was a story of terror that would haunt him for a lifetime. The deadly voyage of the *Daniel J. Morrell* is one of Lake Huron's most tragic and remarkable tales. And this is her story.

■ CHAPTER FOUR

THE MORRELL'S WORLD

T he year was 1906. Our president was Teddy Roosevelt, the flag had forty-five stars, and Las Vegas was home to only thirty hardy souls. Just three years earlier, two brothers, Orville and Wilbur Wright, had created and launched a strange flying machine that would, in 1905, be refined into the world's first airplane.

Life was a daily challenge, full of hardships and inconvenience. On average, people lived to be only 47 years old. More than 90 percent of homes did not have a telephone, and just one in seven had a bathtub. There were only 8,000 cars nationwide compared with the 204 million today. There was no such thing as Scotch tape or crossword puzzles. No Mother's Day or Father's Day. And television would not be invented for another forty years!

The United States was indeed a very different place from the country we now know.

Teachers earned only about $325 each year, less than half of what today's average worker earns in *one week!* And education was different, too. Only 6 percent of all Americans graduated from high school, whereas today over 80 percent have a diploma. Even medical care suffered since 90 percent of all doctors never even went to college.

16 ■ Deadly Voyage

The top causes of death were pneumonia, influenza, tuberculosis, and diarrhea. And natural disasters took a toll as well. In fact, on April 18, 1906, one of America's most devastating tragedies occurred in San Francisco. At about five o'clock in the morning, a horrible rumbling stirred people out of their peaceful sleep. The earth's violent shaking was felt all the way down to Los Angeles and as far north as Oregon. When the smoke finally cleared and the crumbling buildings silenced the victims' screams, the great San Francisco earthquake of 1906 left nearly 75 percent of the city's population homeless. But the homeless were the survivors. The death toll was mind-boggling. At least 3,000 people perished on that tragic day.

This was the world that the *Daniel J. Morrell* entered when she was launched in September 1906, five months after the San Francisco earthquake. The *Morrell* was built for the Cambria Steamship Company of Cleveland by West Bay Shipbuilding of West Bay City, Michigan. Named after a top-level executive of the successful Cambria Iron Company of Johnstown, Pennsylvania, the *Morrell* represented the best of the new Great Lakes freighters. At an imposing 603 feet long, on her end the *Morrell* would extend nearly two-thirds the height of the Eiffel Tower, which at that time was the world's tallest structure.

In 1862, in the midst of the Civil War, the Cambria Iron Company operated the largest rail mill in the nation. It employed 2,500 men at the rail mill and 1,500 at coal and ore mines. The company was led by three men: Charles Wood was its president, Edward Y. Townsend was vice president, and Daniel J. Morrell was the general superintendent and manager. Five years later, Morrell was elected to the U.S. House of Representatives as a Republican from Pennsylvania. He died on August 20, 1885, and is buried in Grandview Cemetery in Johnstown, Pennsylvania.

In 1908, the Cambria Steamship Company came under the management of the M. A. Hanna Company. Shipping companies commonly use colors to identify the ships in their fleet, so the *Morrell*'s hull was repainted black and white, the Hanna company colors. Typical of the Hanna ships, the *Morrell*'s smokestack was also painted black. She remained under Hanna management until 1926.

In 1927 the *Morrell's* owner, still the Cambria Steamship Company, resumed the ship's management. From 1930 until the tragic wreck in 1966, the Bethlehem Transportation Company managed the *Morrell*, and the Cambria Steamship Company retained ownership. Under Bethlehem's management, the *Morrell* was given livelier hull colors of red and white, sporting a bright yellow smokestack. The *Morrell* kept Bethlehem's colors for the remainder of her career. In fact, in 1963, the Cambria Steamship Company joined the Great Lakes Steamship Division of the Bethlehem Steel Company of Cleveland.

The *Morrell* was initially equipped with a 1,878-horsepower engine that was powered by two coal-fired boilers. Her gross tonnage was 7,239 and increased in 1944 to an amazing 7,763 tons. She was huge! Everything was supersized on this marvelous work of early twentieth-century shipping technology. Even the steam whistle, attached to her smokestack, weighed hundreds of pounds.

The *Morrell's* massive hull was held together by huge, riveted steel plates. The ship contained eighteen cargo hatches, which can be counted by looking straight down the spar (working) deck. The hatches were covered by sliding plates that were thirty-six feet long and twelve-feet wide. Each cover was secured by huge clamps, standard for the big ore carriers.

On the *Morrell's* fiftieth birthday, she was given a great present. It was a brand new, state-of-the-art Skinner engine. The Skinner was lighter than the old engine and able to crank out an incredible 3,200 horsepower. Powered by a much bigger shaft with a fourteen-inch diameter and a five-bladed propeller (instead of four), the *Morrell* could now go three miles per hour faster. While this may not sound like much, it could mean a 20 to 25 percent increase in speed for the hauling giant.

The *Morrell* was, of course, outfitted with required safety equipment. This included two steel lifeboats in the aft (rear) that could each hold twenty-one crewmen. There were also two life rafts that could each hold a maximum fifteen men. One was secured at the bow (front) between the third and fourth hatches, and the other was on the stern (rear). An emergency alarm was located in the *Morrell's* pilothouse, along with radar and two radios. A radio telephone enabled the captain or first mate to communicate with other ships and with the shipping company's radio dispatcher. The radio could be operated from either the pilothouse or the captain's cabin.

During her first years on the lakes, the *Morrell* was unquestionably a giant among freighters, making record hauls. In fact, one of her early crewmen, a deckhand named L. G. Webb, was only a boy of sixteen in 1908 when he served on the *Morrell*. He proudly claimed that at one time the *Morrell* held a record for hauling the largest load of iron ore, more than 12,000 tons, enough to fill 120 railcars or more than 450 trucks. He remembered hauling a load of coal right on the spar deck that was piled twenty-four feet high! Despite serving only one season aboard the great ship, Webb mentioned in a newspaper interview that "we had some pretty close calls ourselves that year. The compass always gave us trouble."

This trouble may have been the reason why the *Morrell* was selected as the first freighter to get a high-tech navigational instrument called a gyrocompass. This is an ingenious device that detects north by combining the earth's rotational pull, friction, and a rapidly spinning wheel.

In 1908, the technology was still in its infancy, but by 1922 history was made when a gyrocompass was installed on the *Morrell* by the Sperry Gyroscope Company. She was the first vessel on the Great Lakes to be so equipped. This was unusual for a freighter since these were more typically found on battleships and destroyers, and only five passenger ocean liners had one. It's a highly accurate navigational system, and the *Morrell*'s original gyrocompass has such historical significance that it can be seen on display at the Smithsonian Institute in Washington, D.C. Today a gyrocompass and its variations are standard equipment on most merchant vessels, as well as other types of ships and aircraft.

Early in her career, the *Morrell* had one serious mishap. In a very dense fog on a Friday the 13th in August 1909, the *Morrell* collided with the *Henry Phipps* in the treacherous waters of Whitefish Point on Lake Superior. This stretch is so dangerous it is known as the "Graveyard of the Great Lakes." The *Phipps* was almost the *Morrell*'s twin, built by the same shipbuilder in the same year. Although the collision of the three-year-olds was costly, fortunately it claimed no lives and did not alter either vessel's career. The *Phipps* continued to sail for seventy more years; the *Morrell's* service ended more abruptly at sixty.

As the decades ticked away, the *Morrell* became a veteran of many storms. One of the worst was the November 18, 1958, storm on Lake Michigan that ripped the *Carl D. Bradley* in two and took with it thirty-three of her crew. On that very night, the *Morrell* was fighting her own battle, enduring the gale-force blasts of Lake Superior. That night, the *Morrell* was lucky. But luck is fickle, and on the Great Lakes, storms keep coming.

Throughout the years that the *Morrell* sailed the Great Lakes, there was another 600-foot giant, the *Edward Y. Townsend*, whose shipping career paralleled that of the *Morrell*. The *Townsend* was launched on August 18, 1906, a month before the *Morrell*. Named after the vice president of the Cambria Iron Company, the *Townsend* was built by the Superior Shipbuilding Company of Superior, Wisconsin. Years later, the *Morrell* and *Townsend* became known as sister ships because they were similarly sized, were operated by the same company, and had the same type of construction. But something else linked these two ships. On a terrifying night in November, they followed the same dangerous route on Lake Huron, communicating with each other through a vicious storm. When the seas eventually calmed, neither ship would sail again.

CHAPTER FIVE

OUTWARD BOUND

O n November 26, 1966, the ore-loaded *Daniel J. Morrell* eased her way into Lackawanna, just a few miles south of the Lake Erie port of Buffalo, New York. Her captain and crew believed that they had reached the end of another long and arduous shipping season. The little town of Lackawanna was home to a Bethlehem Steel plant. Bethlehem Steel was the *Morrell*'s owner and operator, and it was here that, along with her sister ship, the *Edward Y. Townsend*, the *Morrell* waited in line for her turn to be unloaded.

It was Saturday, just two days after Thanksgiving, and the treacherous month of November was almost behind them. When the *Morrell* reached Lackawanna she was a crewman short. On Thanksgiving Day, Hjalmer Edwards, a porter, had come down with a respiratory illness. He was admitted to a hospital when they docked at Sault Ste. Marie, Michigan, on Lake Superior. Edwards was a twenty-five-year veteran of the Great Lakes, and at sixty-one, he was only a year older than his ship. When the *Morrell* departed, Edwards was too ill to travel and remained in the hospital. He did not know it then, but it was the luckiest illness he ever had.

Nearly one-fourth of the crew came from the Buffalo area, and after finally reaching Lackawanna, they were more than ready to celebrate the holidays with family and friends. Except for short visits now and then, children had not seen their fathers much in the preceding months. During these visits, they all knew the reunion would be brief, and that Dad would soon be heading out again. The wives of the seamen were used to running the household and playing the role of single parent, but they had long anticipated this time when the men would finally be home for a few months. The long winter layover would allow everyone to get reacquainted. December was just a few days off, and the kids would soon begin their holiday break. It was a time to rest, relax, and enjoy each other's company.

While the *Morrell's* crew patiently waited to unload so each man could finally be on his separate way, a radio message came in to the pilothouse. There had been a change in plans—and it was not good. One of Bethlehem's big ships had broken down. That meant that there was a lot more taconite ore to be picked up, way over in Taconite Harbor, Minnesota, on the west shore of Lake Superior. The *Morrell* would have to make another run, the crew's thirty-fourth trip of the season. The captain of the *Townsend* had been given the same orders and would follow the *Morrell* to her Minnesota destination.

There was also another reason why these ships had to venture out again. Although the crews of the *Morrell* and the *Townsend* believed their season had ended, they did not know that the season's hauling totals for both ships had come in a little short. So they still owed Bethlehem Steel another run. Needless to say, the crews were very disappointed that they could not go home immediately and join their families for the holidays.

The trip would be long for the two old freighters. They would have to travel the length of Lake Erie, go all the way up Lake Huron, and then clear across to the western shore of Lake Superior. And that was just the first half of the journey, picking up the load of taconite pellets used for making steel. It was almost December, and the men found themselves once again having to face the dangers of the lakes.

The master of the *Morrell* was Arthur I. Crawley of Rocky River, Ohio, and this was his first year as a captain. Crawley, the son of a Cleveland butcher, had earned his "masters papers" years before, but he had not decided to serve as a captain until this year. An experienced seaman, the forty-seven-year-old bachelor had served twenty-nine years on the freighters. The youngest of seven children, Crawley signed on to the freighter *Lebanon* the day after he graduated from high school. Interestingly enough, the first ship that he was assigned to as captain was the *Lebanon,* the same ship he had set foot on back when he was eighteen.

As the shipping season progressed, it turned out that the *Morrell* needed a new captain, since her captain of two years, William Hull, stepped down in August. Captain Hull had a long history with the *Morrell,* serving as her second mate back in 1958 when she survived the terrible November storm that sank the *Bradley.* Hull believed that Captain Crawley would be taking the helm of a ship that was in good shape. Except for some minor leaking, which Hull did not think significant enough to report to Bethlehem Steel, the ship was in good working order.

When the opportunity presented itself to serve as master of the *Morrell,* Captain Crawley accepted the job. Although he had chosen the life of a sailor for himself, Arthur Crawley was not one to impose his choices on others. In fact, he did quite the opposite. His sister once said, "My brother never wanted my boys to go on a boat, even in the summer. He said it was a very lonesome life."

The *Morrell*'s disappointed crew was coming to terms with their obligation to Bethlehem Steel to make one last cargo pickup and delivery. Although they were supposed to head out of port at about 11:00 P.M., some of them thought they had enough time for a shore leave before the journey to Minnesota. Two young deckwatchmen, twenty-six-year-old Dennis Hale and his friend, twenty-one-year-old John Groh, believed that they could make a quick drive home and get back in time to catch the *Morrell* before she left Buffalo late that evening. Hale was at the wheel, racing to Erie, Pennsylvania, where Groh's parents lived. From there, Hale would have to make good time to his home in Ashtabula, Ohio, to see his wife and their four children.

At a husky six feet, two inches, and 220 pounds, Dennis Hale was a big, strong guy. Formerly a chef at the Ashtabula Hotel in Ohio, Hale had been working on freighters for only three years. Even though the money was good, his wife, Bertha, who was twenty-nine, begged him to quit. Both of them were well aware of the dangers of sailing these lakes and feared the terrible storms that could blow up without warning. Dennis had promised her that this would be his last season.

The *Morrell*'s cargo of ore had been unloaded and she was ready to travel in ballast, carrying thousands of tons of water in her tanks. This ballast provided stability, which was especially important because Lake Erie had been getting rougher as the evening progressed. At 11:00 P.M. Captain Crawley checked his watch and saw that it was time to leave the safety of port and venture out into Lake Erie. The *Morrell* was outward bound, heading straight into the uncertainty of November's waters. Her planned course would take her across Lake Erie, up the length of Lake Huron, and finally over to Superior's far western shore, where she would load up at Taconite Harbor. If there were no delays and all went well, they would arrive at Minnesota by nine o'clock on Tuesday night, November 29.

When John Groh and Dennis Hale returned to the dock at Lackawanna a few minutes after eleven, they could not believe their eyes. They saw the *Morrell* sailing out of port. The ship had left without them! Not to be denied a nice end-of-the-season bonus that the last voyage would bring, the men radioed Captain Crawley from the Coast Guard Station in Buffalo. After apologizing for their tardiness, they told him they could meet up at Mullen Dock, the *Morrell*'s first fueling stop, near Windsor, Ontario. The captain agreed, and the two men, not wanting to miss their ship a second time, convinced a friend to drive them to Windsor.

At 3:10 A.M., four hours after the *Morrell*'s departure, the *Edward Y. Townsend*, her sister ship, departed Buffalo for the same Minnesota destination of Taconite Harbor.

At the time, the sixty-year-old *Morrell* and *Townsend* were two of the oldest operating ships on the lakes. For many decades, they had been reliable carriers of coal, limestone, and taconite. Bethlehem Steel considered these two old workhorses to be in excellent shape for their age.

The similarities between the two did not end with the ships. Captain

Crawley of the *Morrell* and Thomas J. Connelly, master of the *Townsend,* were about the same age. They were seasoned sailors, each serving a quarter of a century on the Great Lakes. With their final journey underway, the two captains were confident that their ships would carry them safely across the great water.

At nine o'clock on Sunday morning, Captain Crawley was required to make his morning report to Bethlehem Steel's dispatcher in Cleveland. Using his radio telephone, Crawley informed Art Dobson, the chief dispatcher, that he expected to reach Detroit by about six or seven o'clock that evening. Nine hours later, it was clear that the *Morrell* would not make it that far due to bad weather. They ended up dropping anchor at six o'clock in the Detroit River, just south of Detroit. Knowing the importance of keeping the company informed of any schedule changes, Crawley dutifully radioed his position in to the dispatcher.

Although the dispatcher knew of the *Morrell*'s decision to drop anchor before reaching Detroit, two men had not been told. Dennis Hale and John Groh, the two crewmen who missed the departure in Buffalo, were determined to make it to the fueling station well ahead of their ship. Expecting the *Morrell* to come in early in the evening, Hale and Groh made sure they would be there in the afternoon, hours ahead of the ship's anticipated arrival. However, because the bad weather delayed the *Morrell,* they would end up waiting sixteen hours before they could board.

That Sunday night at about eleven, while the *Morrell* was still anchored, the *Townsend* passed her. The two captains spoke to each other on the radio. They talked about the bad weather they expected to encounter on Lake Huron in the next day or two. Five hours later, at four o'clock on Monday morning, Captain Connelly of the *Townsend* approached Stag Island in the St. Clair River and dropped anchor, hoping for the weather to calm a bit.

When the *Morrell* finally pulled into Mullen Dock near Windsor at about seven in the morning, John Groh and Dennis Hale were still patiently waiting. While the big steamship took on a couple hundred tons of coal for fuel, the two men boarded and were immediately expected to perform their work duties. It was 7:30 A.M. when the *Morrell* had finished taking on her fuel and steamed her way out into Lake Huron. Lucky for Hale, his 4:00 to 8:00 A.M. shift was about to end by the time he boarded. That meant he could catch a few hours of sleep. Groh's shift, however, was just beginning and would last until noon, so he did not have the luxury of going to bed. Instead, he went right to work.

At eight o'clock Monday morning, the *Morrell* was beginning her northerly journey up the length of mighty Lake Huron. The winds were picking up, and the late November storm was worsening. At this very moment, Hale's friend John Groh and the rest of the *Morrell*'s crew had less than a day to live.

CHAPTER SIX

THE WITCH OF NOVEMBER

arly on Monday morning, November 28, while the *Morrell* slowly lumbered up the Lake Huron coast, Michigan was being socked hard by a blizzard that would become the worst snowstorm in a decade. The next day, a headline in the *Chicago Tribune* trumpeted in giant bold letters: "1,000 MAROONED BY SNOW!" This was serious weather. Fierce north winds blew the falling snow into drifts that were seven feet high. Ten thousand homes were without any electricity, and whole communities lost contact with the outside world.

One such place was the little town of Curtis, in Michigan's Upper Peninsula. All 1,500 residents had been cut off from everyone else for two days. Not so much as a snowplow had made it to the imperiled town. It was almost surreal to see motorized ski sleds and snowmobiles roaring over the *tops* of cars buried beneath the snow that blanketed Curtis.

The storm served Michigan's Upper Peninsula a whopping sixteen inches of snow, and the winds were clocked at seventy miles per hour, creating mammoth snowdrifts. It was the witch of November that came blowing with a vengeance across land and water. Motorists and travelers were marooned, and highways became clogged with drifts that loomed like small mountains as cars tried to navigate the dangerous whiteout conditions. Many of those stranded were returning from the Thanksgiving holiday, traveling back to school or back home from visiting relatives.

From the Upper Peninsula, the storm moved southeastward, where freezing rain became the most serious threat. Soon this turned to snow as well, and the residents of the Lower Peninsula (Michigan's "Mitten") found themselves locked in a blizzard that a state trooper described as "deteriorating by the hour." It was so bad that state police had to travel on snowmobiles. The storm continued to blow eastward, across the southern shore of Lake Erie, moving across Ohio, dropping eight inches on Pennsylvania, and continuing to blow its wrath to Buffalo, on Erie's eastern shore. Also hit hard were West Virginia (ten inches of snow), and even North Carolina received an amazing sixteen inches.

On that same Monday, a car ferry named the *City of Midland* was washed onto a sandbar off of Michigan's west coastal tourist town of Ludington after she encountered twelve-foot waves—stranding 128 passengers and 56 crew members. Fortunately, no one was hurt. The passengers just had to wait patiently for their rescue as the storm raged outside their staterooms.

That evening, at about eight-thirty Captain Crawley of the *Morrell* and Captain Connelly of the *Townsend* spoke by radio about the weather. Connelly reported that the *Townsend* was up to Harbor Beach, making surprisingly good time at thirteen miles per hour. Harbor Beach is a tiny town located on the northeast shore of Michigan's Thumb. The *Morrell* was a little bit ahead, but no one knows exactly where. We just know she was traveling north along the eastern shore of the Thumb. Both captains commented on the wind shift that had occurred. The west winds were now coming from the north and were clocked at thirty-five miles per hour. Since the ships were sailing north, the wind shift was significant. They were now sailing directly into the wind. And that was not all. Both captains estimated the waves at eight feet and getting bigger all the time. With increasing winds and bigger waves, this storm was rapidly escalating into a full-fledged Great Lakes November blow.

After just twenty minutes of sailing into the teeth of the north wind, the *Townsend*'s former pace of thirteen miles per hour had been reduced to just five miles per hour. Connelly had the engines powering at what would have produced ten miles per hour on normal seas, but the *Townsend* could not counter the force of the unrelenting wind.

It was around nine-thirty when Dennis Hale decided to go to bed. His watchman shift would begin at four in the morning, so he knew he had to get some sleep. Without talking to anyone, he readied himself for bed. While he got ready, he could sense that the sea was getting rougher. His quarters were on the ship's forward starboard (front right), within earshot of the *Morrell*'s gigantic anchors. As he closed his eyes, he could feel that the ship was rolling enough to cause the anchors to clunk loudly against the ship's bow.

By ten o'clock that evening, Captains Crawley and Connelly talked again, discussing the increasingly serious conditions. North winds were blowing hard at fifty miles per hour, a gale-force storm. In just ninety minutes, the waves increased to twelve feet. But things would get much worse. Within a few short hours, the waves would nearly double in height!

Captain Connelly knew that his ship, now just eight miles north of Harbor Beach, was handling the adverse conditions well, but he was experiencing some rolling. Sleeping was tough for the crew as the old ship rocked, creaked, and groaned under the stress of the heavy seas. In fact, for the safety of the crew, Connelly restricted their movement up and down the ship's deck for the next twenty-four hours. He knew that in storms like this, the *Townsend* could broach, that is, swing out or spin in the wind and sea, taking on big water from the side. Ultimately, it could be enough to capsize even a giant vessel like the *Townsend*.

At 11:15 P.M., after enduring these treacherous seas for a little more than an hour, the two captains once again made radio contact. Waves were growing higher by the hour, and winds increased to fifty-five miles per hour. On land, gale winds like these were strong enough to uproot trees and cause serious damage to buildings. Still, the rugged *Townsend* was weathering the storm. Connelly told Crawley that he was hoping to make it up to the safe shelter of Thunder Bay, on the east shoreline of Michigan's Mitten and close to the town of Alpena. There the ship could anchor and wait out the blow. The other option was to turn back and go south to the harbor town of Port Huron. Connelly believed that heading north to Thunder Bay was safer than turning around and risking capsizing by getting caught in the trough of a wave.

While the two captains were talking, another voice crackled over the radio. It was Captain James Van Buskirk of the 612-foot *Benson Ford*. He was southbound on Lake Huron, sailing from northern Lake Michigan and loaded with 10,000 tons of iron ore. He had just come from Huron's Thunder Bay, and he advised the two captains it would offer them safe refuge. When he signed off, Van Buskirk was sure that the two captains had agreed to plot a course for Thunder Bay. It would be a long run through one of the fiercest gales ever witnessed on this lake. Could they make it?

About thirty minutes had passed and it was now ten minutes before midnight. The *Townsend* was close to the Pointe Aux Barques Lighthouse, north of Harbor Beach. At this point, the winds were so powerful they almost stopped the ship in her tracks. Pushing with all her might, she was able to make only two miles per hour, slower than a person walking. For the next two hours, the *Morrell* also only made about three or four miles, so she too was held virtually at a standstill.

Tom Connelly found the weather to be a good deal more serious than earlier weather forecasts had indicated. It was far worse than the lower two-thirds of Lake Huron that he had just navigated. Connelly later told the Coast Guard Investigation Board that he had never before seen seas so wild and dangerous on the Lakes. In fact, it was so bad that both he and Van Buskirk of the *Benson Ford* testified that they could not have lowered their lifeboats.

Shortly after midnight Captain Connelly spoke briefly to Captain Crawley. Both skippers had been driven off course by waves that had increased to twenty feet. Desperately trying to maintain their ships' positions, they got off their radio phones to focus on the survival of their imperiled, storm-tossed ships. This was the last contact anyone would have with the *Daniel J. Morrell*.

For the next two hours the *Morrell* was struggling for survival. The 65 mph winds continued to batter her head on, reducing the ship's progress to a mere crawl. Sixty years old and a veteran of many Great Lakes storms, the aging giant's hull groaned as mountainous waves smashed across her bow. The monster waves dumped tons of white water on her spar deck. The *Morrell*'s bow dipped downward and then pitched upward, rolling side to side and popping rivets off the steel plates of her hull as she tried to hold her own against the sea. Each time the *Morrell*'s bow plunged downward into the frothy sea, the giant rear propeller rose out of the water!

At 1:45 A.M., Captain Connelly tried to bring up the *Morrell* on his ship's radio. No luck. Just dead air. Over the past two hours he had observed a wind shift from the north to northeast. The screaming 65 mph winds were now near hurricane force and blowing up waves a towering twenty-five feet high. Waves this powerful can lift a whole house off of its foundation and wash it away. Despite these horrendous conditions, Connelly was able to keep his ship on her northbound route, but the *Townsend* was taking a brutal pounding, dramatically rolling and pitching her way through the high seas. Like the *Morrell,* the *Townsend* repeatedly took monster waves across her bow, her deck awash with an icy weight that pitched her nose downward into the mighty turbulence.

Why did the master of the *Morrell* fail to respond to the *Townsend*'s radio call? Was there a problem with her radio antenna? Was Captain Crawley too busy to talk, trying to make his way through the storm? In previous radio communications, the *Morrell*'s skipper had never mentioned mechanical problems. As the Coast Guard later noted, Captain Crawley "had not reported any difficulty with his vessel, radios, equipment, structure, operations, machinery, or problems of any kind except weather conditions and the difficulty of holding the vessel into the sea."

Two hours later, at 3:45 A.M., Connelly tried again to contact the *Morrell.* Still no answer. Not wanting to imagine the worst, Connelly attributed the silence to radio problems. This was not at all unreasonable. After all, the *Townsend* never had the *Morrell* on her radar, so he did not see the ship drop from sight. Perhaps ice from the snowstorm and high winds had caused problems with the *Morrell*'s radio antenna. Although Connelly was unsure just how far ahead the *Morrell* was, he estimated the distance to be about twenty miles.

What Captain Connelly did not know was that the eerie radio silence that haunted him in the early morning hours of November 29 was a chilling foreshadowing of the terrible tragedy that would befall the *Daniel J. Morrell* and her crew.

CHAPTER SEVEN

MADNESS AT SEA

I t was early Tuesday morning at approximately two o'clock when Dennis Hale was awakened from his sleep by a loud bang. Half asleep, he guessed it was the sound of the anchor against the ship's bow. He had sailed for three years, and he knew that these freighters could make a lot of noises. After all, she was being knocked around pretty well by the storm. But soon he heard another bang, and this one was even louder. It was so violent the books by his bedside avalanched to the floor. Clearly, this wasn't an anchor knocking against the hull. Something extraordinary was happening. But what? Hale tried to turn on a light, but nothing—no electricity. His fears were confirmed, for as he sat on the edge of his bed, the ship's alarm sounded. In complete darkness and wearing only his boxer shorts, he grabbed his life jacket, hurried down the walkway, and opened the door leading to the spar deck.

On the forward spar deck no lights were working, but he could make out lights far down in the aft section. Then he saw something else—something terrifying. And it was something he could never forget. The *Morrell* was hogging. Hogging is when high seas are so strong they can raise the ship with a powerful heave and then exhale the hull down. Though these freighters are built to allow some flex and movement, excessive rising and falling of the ship's middle—hogging—can place incredible stress on the hull. What Hale saw was the aft section rising high above the deck of the forward section where he was standing. He could hear the sounds of metal rubbing against itself and cracking. Sparks mingled with the flying snow as the electrical cables of the bow snapped, leaving the bow without lights, power, or a radio telephone for an SOS. Unbelievably, this great ship was being bent in two, right before his eyes!

Just then Hale ran into Norman Bragg, a forty-year-old watchman from New York. Without missing a beat, he told Hale that they needed to make it to the raft because he thought the ship was breaking up. Hale knew that Bragg was a veteran of these seafaring wars. Back in 1953, when he was about Hale's age, Bragg had survived a Lake Superior storm that sank the *Henry Steinbrenner*. That night, seventeen of his crewmates had lost their lives.

Both Bragg and Hale knew the situation was critical and there was no time to lose. But it was thirty-three degrees outside, and the high water washing up on the deck was like ice. Barefoot and wearing only underwear and a life jacket, Hale needed more clothing, including a coat, pants, and shoes.

Instinctively, he dashed back to his cabin, but there were no lights, and everything was black. Feeling around for his pants, all he could find was his wool peacoat. It was a good thing to have because he needed something warm. In seconds Hale galloped out of his cabin and back to the deck, feeling the icy slush squishing through his bare toes. Clad in his odd emergency gear of a life vest against his skin, boxers, and the peacoat, Hale had to now concentrate on his survival.

He knew right then what he had to do—the ship was breaking up, and he had to try to make it to the forward life raft. His best chance for survival would be to sit aboard the untied raft and hang on while the *Morrell* sank beneath the angry turbulence. He could not see either lifeboat and wondered if they had been lowered. But in this storm and under these conditions, there was no way to use them.

With the freezing wind stinging his face and the sea crashing onto the deck, Hale ran barefoot toward the red life raft on the slippery, snowy deck. In all of the chaos, he saw many of the crew huddled around the life raft, helpless but hopeful. Then he heard someone tell the crewmen to "get on the raft and hold on tight." According to the Coast Guard investigation report, Hale remembered that many "deck personnel, including the Master, First Mate, and Second Mate sat on the raft to await the [ship's] sinking." That meant that a dozen or so men were atop the fifteen-man raft. Constructed of steel pontoons and heavy boards, the raft was too heavy for them to lift and launch, so the men sat and waited for the ship to submerge, setting the raft afloat. During this time, Hale later recalled, no one gave emergency instructions concerning the lifesaving equipment, such as the flares or the flare gun. There was not much talking. Each man waited silently. These would be their final thoughts, their last minutes alive.

Shivering on the raft, Hale saw that many of the others were also partially dressed, and, like him, they were all wearing their life jackets. Tensely the men awaited their fate. Norm Bragg and young John Groh (the friend who boarded late with Hale) even tied themselves to the raft so they would not be tossed off if a rogue wave should suddenly hurl them into the sea. But this did not save them. Within just minutes both men would be dead. Back in Erie, Groh's mother would wait in vain for news of her son.

While nervously waiting on the raft, Dennis learned that no distress signal had been transmitted since the bow's electrical power had gone out when the lines were severed in the breakup. From that moment on, no radio contact was possible. Still, they believed the *Townsend* and perhaps another ship were in the vicinity, and so they held out hope that flares would be spotted. Captain Crawley thought it best to wait until the raft entered the water before opening the storage locker that held the flares. At that time, flares could be launched skyward.

Looking down ship toward the stern which was still lit, Hale could see only one crew member, Oiler Don Worcester, eerily standing with his ever-present oilcan, staring out into the darkness. Hale remembers that Worcester looked as if nothing unusual was happening. Perhaps he was frozen with shock. Glancing above into the blackness, just below the pilothouse, Hale could make out a light and another familiar face. It was Third Mate Ernie Marcotte from Pontiac, Michigan. He appeared as a ghostlike figure, standing motionlessly in the shadows, holding his flashlight. Marcotte could see that the raft was at capacity, and he made no effort to come down and squeeze aboard. He remained there with his flashlight, standing guard over the dying vessel.

Worcester's home was Columbia Falls, Maine, where he lived with his wife and four children. Marcotte was sixty-two, married and close to retirement. It was Hale's last glimpse of the two men. Their bodies would be lost until the next spring, washed ashore on a Canadian island, seventy miles away.

Despite the madly raging sea and the dire circumstances, no one panicked. Things were remarkably orderly, not chaotic as one might expect. The men's faces were set with the grim determination of those about to face a test where stakes are highest—life itself.

Straining to see what was happening, Hale could see that the ship was cracking on a line from the starboard side (right) around hatches 11 and 12 and snaking all the way across to port side (left). No question about it, she was breaking in half right before their eyes. Hale later described the breakup, "I heard this noise and I looked over my shoulder towards the stern and I could see the one-inch steel plate just tearing like a piece of paper. That's something that will never leave my memory." He also noticed that the starboard side was sitting a good deal lower than the whole aft section—a twisting of the forward part of the ship. This rubbing of metal against metal produced a flash of sparks.

Just then a blast of steam belched from the enlarging gap between bow and stern, and suddenly the ship separated, transformed into two halves, one dying, the other still in motion and breathing steam. The broken and helpless bow section, that still held the raft on which Hale and his shipmates clung to life, was now completely at the mercy of the wind and sea. The stern, however, took on a life of her own, her boilers still puffing and gasping steamy breath. As the steam escaped from the boilers, it made a horrible scream in the darkness like an unleashing of terrible demons. The missing front half of the ship had no effect on the powerful engine, which still drove the stern onward. Amazingly, in the midst of this frightening madness at sea, the ghostly stern began ramming her own bow broadside, almost like something possessed!

Hale and his shipmates were atop the raft on that sinking forward section, holding on for life itself. Surprisingly, there was still no panic. The stern powered herself over to the bow's port side, heading straight for a broadside hit, exactly where the men were clinging to the raft on the spar deck. The stern's cavernous cargo hold, with her lights still glowing brightly, looked very much alive and was now coming directly toward them. To Hale it looked like the "gaping mouth of a monster that was about to devour me."

The bow began to angle down more steeply into the black turbulence as the water rushed into the gaping hull. As the water flooded the open cargo hold, the huge front section angled below the surface, pulling the bow heavenward, like a three-hundred-foot mountain of steel. Their raft was suddenly slammed by a huge wave, throwing her and all the men over the starboard side of the sinking bow. The men were chaotically and unmercifully tossed in all directions. Many were wearing practically nothing as they were hurled through the frigid air and cast into the bone-chilling forty-four-degree waters. Dennis was fully immersed in towering twenty-five foot waves and blizzard winds that blasted him at sixty-five miles per hour.

Dragged to the depths of a watery darkness, Hale opened his eyes and could make out his own air bubbles rising. This allowed him to get his bearings, to know which way was up. Following his bubbles, he pulled himself up, up, and with one final thrust he broke the surface, hurling his body like a missile six feet above the water and into the icy air!

Emerging into the blackness of the November storm, Hale looked around and spotted the glowing of a bright, white light. It was the raft's water-activated carbide safety lantern. The raft was thirty or forty feet away, and she was empty. It would be difficult but he knew that he had to make it over to that raft, through the deep troughs and twenty-five-foot seas. Each time he was lifted to the top of a wave he could see the raft, but when he rolled down into its trough, she disappeared. Swimming blindly toward where he imagined her to be, he finally made it to the raft.

When he reached the raft, there were now two men aboard. They were deckhands Art Stojek and John Cleary, Jr. The forty-one-year-old Stojek, wearing only his light pajamas and a life jacket, appeared to be dazed. In addition to his life jacket, Cleary had on jeans and a sweatshirt. Cleary was the second youngest man on board, just twenty and single. Soon after the men dragged Hale onto the pitching raft, a fourth man was pulled aboard. He was Charles Fosbender, a wheelsman from St. Clair, Michigan. "Fuzzy," as they called him, was an experienced seaman, sailing nine years for Bethlehem Steel. Although fully dressed and wearing a life jacket, he was freezing and drenched to the skin, just like the others. When the other men asked how he was, Fuzzy said he was okay. He did not know—probably because he was in shock—that his chest and shoulders had been crushed when the bow threw him overboard. He endured incredible pain from his injuries, yet throughout the whole ordeal, the *Morrell*'s soft-spoken wheelsman never complained.

The tragedy that unfolded had not taken long. From the sounding of the alarm to the sudden and deadly immersion, eight endlessly painful minutes had passed—minutes when every man knew that his fate was about to be sealed.

Before being thrown overboard, Hale had seen no one in the water. He thought that the stern's raft was still sitting on the stern section which remained afloat. Neither lifeboat had been freed either. The four shivering men, wearing little more than their life jackets, were now huddled on the *Morrell*'s only life-saving equipment available—a solitary raft. Fifteen minutes after Hale and his shipmates were thrown overboard, the *Morrell*'s bow slipped beneath the towering waves, swallowed by the angry lake.

The little raft had been blown about two hundred yards from where the bow went under, and the stern was chugging along through the big water with her lights still on, now between a half mile and a mile away, powering herself blindly into the storm, despite missing three hundred feet of her body! The *Morrell* was now like an animal that continues to run even after her head has been cut off. The four men on the raft never saw the stern sink.

Once the bow sank and they gathered their wits about them, the men could see no one else in the water. No cries for help, no bodies, nothing. Hale searched for the parachute flares and handheld flares that were kept in the raft's storage locker. Surely someone would see the red, fiery sparks hanging and then falling from the sky like fireworks. How disappointed they must have been to discover that two of the flares had been lost overboard when the raft was washed off the bow. There were, however, a couple of flares left, and Hale carefully loaded the stubby flare gun and was able to send up two distress signals. But then the gun broke in two, the handle and the barrel. Hale cleverly held them together and fired off the rest of the parachute flares. With cloudy skies and snow blowing all around, nighttime visibility was limited, and the *Townsend* was probably fifteen to twenty miles away.

The four crewmen, Art Stojek, Fuzzy Fosbender, young Jack Cleary, and Dennis Hale, were now shipmates of a very different sort. They had been thrust into a foreign world—from the familiarity of their six-hundred-foot freighter to a free-floating raft, from the warmth and security of their cabins to the freezing and unrelenting attacks of nature at her most cruel. They were in a life-and-death struggle in the pitch dark of the early morning hours of November 29. Not only did no one know where they were, but no one even knew that the *Morrell* had broken in two. Wildly tossed and blindly carried at the whim of the sea, the four sailors huddled together at one end of the raft to share their body warmth.

At the time of the *Morrell*'s breakup, no one aboard knew that the Coast Guard cutter *Acacia* was just twenty miles away. Lieutenant Commander Charles Millradt much later realized that if only the *Morrell* had sent out a distress call, the cutter could have made it to the scene. And rather than performing the grisly task of collecting bodies out of the lake, as the *Acacia* did two days later, the cutter could have possibly saved the lives of the *Morrell*'s crew. But the breakup and loss of electrical power to the bow changed all that. The instant the hull began to crack, communications were disabled and no SOS could be sent. Instead, at about three o'clock in the morning, the *Acacia* headed off toward Thunder Bay to respond to an SOS sent by the German freighter *Nordmeer.* Another life-and-death drama was being played out miles away across the giant lake. Eight crewmen had been stranded on the ship for days, and she was breaking up offshore of the town of Alpena.

With no distress signal, no call for help, no SOS, and no one who even knew that they were out in the middle of this great lake at its most dangerous, what hope could there be for the four sailors who were lucky enough to board the raft? How long would they have to endure this brutal and deadly ordeal? Perhaps a better question is, how long *could* they hold on?

CHAPTER EIGHT

CHAOS!

During the *Morrell*'s tragic struggle, chaos reigned up and down the Huron coast. From the early morning hours of November 29, calls were coming in about ships that were struggling in the late-November gale. But no one had any idea of what was happening to the *Morrell*. Captain Connelly of the *Townsend* had last communicated with the *Morrell*'s Captain Crawley just after midnight. In fact, no one was even sure if they had seen the doomed ship on radar. Some time after one o'clock in the morning, the skipper of the *Benson Ford,* James Van Buskirk, was sailing southward with a tailwind of sixty miles per hour when he picked up on his radar what he thought was a passing ship. Was she the *Townsend,* or could she have been the *Morrell* just before she went down?

At 1:45 A.M., close to when the *Morrell* was breaking up, the 592-foot *Kinsman Independent,* fully loaded with coal, found herself in an extraordinarily dangerous predicament near Pointe Aux Barques Lighthouse, just north of Harbor Beach. Captain Zernie Newman was valiantly trying to hold his ship in the sea, but the incredible force of the sixty-mile-per-hour winds actually spun her around, reversing the course of a huge freighter! After being blown off course, the imperiled vessel was caught in a trough between wave crests, unable to get out. Maneuvering this giant against the forces of nature, Newman ran the risk of capsizing, sending him and his crew to Huron's icy depths. For four grueling minutes the *Kinsman*'s captain and crew were trapped. No matter what he tried, Captain Newman could not free his ship from the trough. Finally, he was somehow able to reverse his course and allow the tailwind to blow him southward to Port Huron. After Newman and his crew returned to safety he said that this was the most vicious storm he had ever experienced on Lake Huron, far worse than any of the weather forecasts had predicted.

Throughout the night, ships that were attempting to weather the storm changed their plans, altered their routes, and headed southward in search of calmer seas. At the same time the *Kinsman Independent* was struggling for survival, several other big ships were in the vicinity of the Pointe Aux Barques Lighthouse. Most turned back, taking great winds at their stern and seeking a safe harbor to drop anchor. The *Howard L. Shaw*, *Robert Hobson*, *Henry Steinbrenner*, and *Harry Coulby* all turned around when they saw how the seas and winds tossed them about. The northbound *Shaw*, a 451-foot Canadian freighter, was blown so violently that the ship's wheel spun out of control, useless against the raging sea. Twice she tried to continue her northward journey but failed. As with the *Kinsman Independent*, the sea and wind turned the northbound *Shaw* around completely so she was now facing south. Captain L. D. Jones of the *Shaw* described the terror as being "spun around like a top."

Things were no better for the big coal-carrying *Robert Hobson*. Her captain, Charles D. Finch, later testified that the waters of Lake Huron that night were "the worst continuously heavy seas I've ever been through." Like the *Morrell* and *Townsend*, the 586-foot *Hobson* was northbound, some miles behind the *Morrell*. She was battling the sea about three miles north of Harbor Beach. At 2:30 A.M., just a half hour after the *Morrell* broke in two, Captain Finch managed to turn his ship around. He did not believe it was safe to continue a northern passage under such treacherous conditions, so the *Hobson* joined the caravan of lakers heading for the refuge of Port Huron.

Like the *Hobson*, the *Henry Steinbrenner* (not to be confused with the ship by the same name that was lost on Lake Superior back in 1953) attempted to turn around in the churning waters. The skipper of the *Steinbrenner* took eight nail-biting minutes to negotiate the seas in an effort to reverse his northbound course and return to Port Huron. Luckily, he finally managed the dangerous maneuver.

After a twenty-foot wall of water swept across her bow, the 5,000-horse-power *Harry Coulby* was also no match for this storm. Sailing north between Port Sanilac and Harbor Beach, the captain was well aware of the increasingly bad conditions ahead at Pointe Aux Barques Lighthouse. Like the others, the 615-footer joined the southbound exodus to the safety of Port Huron.

The captain of the northward bound *Fred A. Manske* had the same thought as the other skippers. By the time he reached Pointe Aux Barques Lighthouse, he, too, wanted to head south to Port Huron. The 504-foot *Manske* was getting knocked around in a frightful manner. But she was a self-unloader, meaning she had a giant boom on her main deck. The captain feared that the ship's heavy self-unloading apparatus might throw off the topside balance and swamp or capsize his vessel. Because of this danger, the captain had to weigh the risk of reversing his course against continuing in the face of the north wind. He continued north safely.

The dark morning hours of November 29 were indeed chaotic on Lake Huron. In addition to Captains Connelly, Newman, and Finch, others would later testify that Lake Huron's deadly storm of 1966 was one of the worst they had ever witnessed. Imagine winds so mighty they can take a freighter that is the length of two football fields and spin her completely around. While the vicious winds howl, waves two stories high slam head on into the ship, forcing her into violent fits of pitching and rolling. Holding their own against the sea on this frightening night was all these captains could hope for.

About an hour after the *Morrell* broke up, still another drama was unfolding off of Michigan's eastern coast. Twelve miles out from the coastal town of Alpena, a stranded ship was trapped on a reef by high winds and twenty-foot waves. The *Nordmeer*, a steel-carrying German freighter, was grounded on Thunder Bay Shoal, holding her captain and seven-man crew captive. For nine days, Lake Huron's massive waves relentlessly battered the hapless ship, eventually cracking her hatches and leaving the ship for dead. In the early morning hours of November 29, the ship began breaking up, and the captain knew they would have to evacuate. But how?

At 3:00 A.M., Captain Ernst-George Steinbeck of the *Nordmeer* radioed the Coast Guard rescue station. His SOS revealed that water had been pouring in through all of the ship's hatches since midnight. About that time the Coast Guard cutter *Acacia* was within just twenty miles of the *Morrell*. The *Acacia*'s commander, Charles Millradt, acknowledged the SOS and sailed northward across stormy Lake Huron to the *Nordmeer*'s position in Thunder Bay Shoal.

As the *Acacia* bravely tried to make her way toward the wreck, the *Nordmeer*'s cabins were flooding, forcing all eight men to wait in the pilothouse for their rescue. Unaware that his message was received, Captain Steinbeck sent up distress flares. Eventually it became clear to the Coast Guard that weather conditions would not allow the *Acacia* to continue her rescue mission. Sailing into seas that crested at twenty-five feet and treacherously high winds, the *Acacia* abandoned her northward path. Desperately seeking shelter, she steered the southerly course of so many others that night, returning to her home port of Port Huron.

The stranded and grounded *Nordmeer* did not have this option. And Captain Steinbeck was waiting anxiously for some indication that his SOS had been heard. Of course, the Coast Guard had received the call, but no ships could reach the *Nordmeer*. Even if the *Acacia* had made it to the scene, she would not have been able to maneuver herself alongside the stricken vessel. The only hope was a helicopter rescue, but gale-force winds gusting to seventy miles per hour made such an attempt too dangerous. How long could the crew of the *Nordmeer* hold on? For hours and hours the helpless German crewmen awaited rescue, hoping the storm would finally exhaust itself and die out.

But the storm did not let up. All morning and into the afternoon, the blizzard pounded away at the rapidly deteriorating freighter. Then, late in the afternoon on November 29, something happened, something miraculous that only nature can do. Without warning, there was an unexpected but greatly welcome calming of the storm. The winds slowed and the snow stopped. It lasted less than half an hour, but this was the opportunity they had all been waiting for. The Coast Guard helicopter co-pilot, Lieutenant Jack Rittichier, described it as if somebody had "waved a magic wand."

Taking full advantage of this momentary calm, the helicopter was sent to the site where it hovered above the stranded ship with the broken back. A daring rescue was about to begin. One at a time each man was hauled up in a dangling basket suspended from the helicopter. The pilot held the helicopter steady with a sure hand, as the wind, though not as strong, rocked it over the lake. The helicopter made two trips to the stricken vessel, carrying four men each time and dropping them off safely onto the deck of the massive Coast Guard icebreaker *Mackinaw*. Amazingly, just as the last man was lifted off the wreck, the snowstorm resumed full force. All of the men on the *Nordmeer* had been rescued—a happy ending on what was a day of tragedy for others. Things were going to get far worse, and there would be considerable loss of life as a result of this storm of storms.

CHAPTER NINE

A NIGHTMARE WITHOUT END

I t was 2:30 A.M. in the frigid darkness of November 29, a half hour after the breakup of the *Morrell*. The last four of the *Morrell*'s crew of twenty-nine were hanging on to the raft, their only life support, and no one knew they were even missing. The freezing air temperature was 33 degrees, the fierce winds were gusting to sixty-five miles per hour, and the icy waves were cresting at a staggering twenty-five feet. In Dennis Hale's own words, "The sea was a terrible rage." Alone and at the mercy of the lake, nobody on the raft knew exactly where they were at this moment. And it was not going to change for hours.

The two younger men, Cleary and Hale, took charge on the raft and were preparing to shoot some flares skyward. Fuzzy Fosbender grabbed a flashlight and started waving it as if to signal someone. The other men couldn't figure out what he was doing. He said he was signaling some lights in the distance. Sure enough, there were lights, and it was a ship! But on closer look, their hearts sank when they realized that those were the lights of the *Morrell*'s stern, still chugging along miles into the distance.

There were as many as seventeen crewmen still aboard the stern as she steamed madly along on her southbound course. They had to know that as soon as the icy water hit those flaming boilers the whole stern would be blown sky high, lighting up the darkness with a horrible explosion that would be seen for miles. Somehow they had to get off. They may have attempted to free one of her lifeboats but could not in the high seas. Then there was the life raft. Could that have been used like the one from the bow section? To avoid being burned in the boiler explosion, many of the remaining crew may have jumped into the stormy seas with their life jackets, only to drown or die of hypothermia. In the end, the *Morrell's* open stern traveled five miles on her own before finally succumbing to the lake.

The four men were on the only thing for miles that could save them— an uncovered, free-floating, pontoon-style raft in the open water. They were at least fifteen miles from the nearest ship or land, and visibility was estimated at only four miles.

Together they huddled in the chilling early morning hours. The sea was still thrashing their tiny raft about like a piece of cork. Frozen to the bone and just barely clinging to life, the drenched foursome tried to ride out each wave to its crest, only to be dropped deep into its trough.

It's not easy to describe what it must have been like, wearing practically nothing, clinging desperately to an open raft in freezing temperatures, and being dragged through towering waves of icy water. Thirty years after the sinking, Dennis Hale put words to this nightmare:

> You go through a thirty footer and you feel like your lungs are going to explode and then you start getting air. Then that sixty mile an hour wind hits you . . . and we'd all just cry out in pain—physical and mental pain. You just don't know what's coming next. And after two or three of those, you don't really care. I know at one point I just kind of let go and I was hoping I'd get washed overboard. Anything was better than what was happening right then.

To the best of their knowledge, they were the only remaining survivors. None of the men knew why the *Morrell* had broken up. Hale wasn't even sure if an SOS had been sent. It had not.

Alone with their thoughts on the raft, the men talked little. Art Stojek must have been wondering why he was even out on a raft in this terrible storm. He was not a sailor. In fact, he had never worked on a boat before he became a deckhand. Recently, life had taken a rough turn for him. Two months before, he had been laid off from his job at Dunlop Tires of Tonawanda, New York, just outside of Buffalo. Stojek was the sole means of support for his wife Cecilia and their four children, Tina, Darlene, Arthur Jr. (Archie), and Joseph, as well as Cecilia's parents, who lived with them. Family meant a lot to him, and he took his responsibilities seriously. For the sake of his family's well-being, Stojek knew what he had to do. Desperate to find work, any work, he signed on as a forty-one-year-old deckhand.

Occasionally the men spoke aloud, mainly Dennis Hale and Jack Cleary. At one point, Cleary asked Hale what their chances were, and Hale replied, "a lot better than the guys who didn't make it to this raft." The two talked a little about their families. Cleary spoke about his father, John Sr., back home in Cleveland. They used to build model railroads together, creating miniature towns out of balsa wood and running imaginary miles of track around the basement through the tiny world the two of them created. As a student at West Tech High in Cleveland, Jack's favorite class had been shop, but his greatest love was working on old cars. Always a creative kid, Jack was interested in doing pretty much anything with his hands, including drawing pictures, for which he had a real talent.

When Cleary asked Hale how many kids he had, he told him about his two stepchildren, Billy (age ten) and Debbie (eight), and the two little girls that he and his wife Bertha had, Cindy (six) and Cathy (four). The two smiled when they said how great it would be to be with their families to celebrate Christmas.

But all of this was just a brief diversion, because the men were so very cold they had to concentrate on staying warm and alive. After twenty minutes on the raft Hale's whole body went numb. In his words, "I suffered so much from the cold I was almost hoping to die." When he reached down to touch his bare legs, he could detect only the slightest twinge. He kept his fingers in his mouth to maintain feeling and to keep them from freezing.

The exhausted men tried to get some sleep on the little raft as she continued to pitch high and low, protecting her precious cargo. Hale was in the middle, lying on his left side. To his left was Fuzzy, a little lower, curled up with his back against Hale's legs. Then there was Stojek, who was just above Fosbender, also with his back to Hale. Cleary was on the far right, lying on his stomach. They remained in this position as water washed over them, draining them of the body heat needed to fend off hypothermia.

During the long hours that followed, Hale drifted in and out of sleep. His emotions tossed him around like the waves he was riding. One minute he would pray for his safety and that of the three men on the raft. The next, he would shout angrily to the heavens. Just as quickly, his tone would change when his thoughts turned to his wife and four children. And then he would pray for all of the rest of the *Morrell*'s crew. Where were they now? Sometimes a wave of hopelessness swallowed him, and he felt like giving up, letting go entirely.

At about seven-thirty in the morning, the faint dawn showed its pale light. Fosbender and Hale looked at Jack Cleary and Art Stojek and beheld their lifeless bodies and blank expressions. Five hours into their ordeal, they had passed away. Fosbender and Hale lay in silence between their two lost shipmates. "You get to know men well when you sail with them," Hale would later say, "and it's hard to see them die." The lake was now less rough, and the two remaining men awaited any sunlight and the warmth it could provide. But it was the beginning of another dark November day. And it would become darker still.

Each man was alone with his thoughts. Fosbender had sailed the lakes for nearly a decade, but this was his first year as part of the *Morrell*'s crew. Although the *Morrell* was considered a giant by most, Fuzzy saw it differently. According to his wife, "He didn't care for the *Morrell* too much because he said it was a much smaller boat; he was used to being on a bigger one." He had previously sailed on the *Johnstown*, nearly one hundred feet longer than the *Morrell*. How could anyone see the *Morrell* as a smaller boat? Since Fuzzy was a wheelsman, working at the helm of these huge freighters, he probably had a different perception of size.

But the survivors' focus had to be on the here and now. Everything came back to survival. Surviving long enough to see the happy faces of family and friends. Life should not end like this—a raft on open water, cold, hungry, and alone.

As afternoon approached, the sun never made much of an appearance. It was a gray day, typical of November. At one point, Hale asked what time it was, and Fuzzy said it was around two. They realized it had been about twelve hours since they were shipwrecked. Twelve hours on these frigid waters on an open raft. Even with a crushed chest and broken shoulders, Fuzzy was somehow able to raise himself up on his elbows and forearms to take a look around. The pain had to be excruciating. He claimed to see land in the distance and very well may have. Hale couldn't move off his left side and was facing away from Fuzzy, looking in the opposite direction, so he could not see anything. Besides, without anyone searching for them or even aware that they were missing, the sight of land in the far distance was not going to help them.

The two men did not say much because they were so weak, thinking only about staying warm. When they did talk, it was usually about family and imagining the mouthwatering meals that would await them at the holidays.

Fosbender was coughing heavily all afternoon. Injuries to his chest and shoulders made each coughing fit even more painful. Late in the afternoon, Hale tried to encourage him, suggesting that maybe they would be spotted. Fuzzy gasped out his response: "Well, they better hurry, because it feels like my lungs are filling up." By four o'clock, fourteen hours after the ship snapped in two, Fuzzy was just barely conscious. Then his body and spirit gave out, and with a final cough, he died.

Hale was now very much alone. Night was falling, and the raft was caked with ice. Throughout the night, he drifted in and out of consciousness, consumed by wild dreams about the ship, the wreck, even of being rescued. He had strange hallucinations of seagulls that attacked him. He talked to the three dead men and cried to the heavens, asking why he was still alive and why the others had died. Each time his mind drifted away, dropping off to sleep or losing consciousness, he knew that he might never wake up.

On November 18, 1958, eight years before the *Morrell* went down, First Mate Elmer Fleming (age forty-three) and Deckwatch Frank Mays (age twenty-six), two crewmen of the *Carl D. Bradley,* had endured fifteen hours on a life raft during a storm on Lake Michigan. They were nearly identical in age to Dennis Hale (twenty-six) and Charlie Fosbender (forty-two). Like Hale and Fosbender, Fleming and Mays had shared their raft with two other shipmates. Of the four men on that raft, only two survived a grueling ordeal that tested the limits of human endurance.

And now there was Dennis Hale, the only man left. How much longer could he hope to hold out for? Another hour? Maybe three or four at most? How about a total of twenty-four hours? That would be unthinkable, certainly not possible. He didn't know it then, but to survive, Dennis Hale, barefoot and without gloves or hat, clad in just his underwear and a coat, would have to endure the lashing snow, gale-force winds, and monster waves longer than anyone could have imagined.

It would take nothing less than a miracle.

CHAPTER TEN

WHERE IS THE *MORRELL?*

By nine o'clock on that cloudy Tuesday morning of November 29, the *Morrell* had been lost for seven hours. But no one knew. No distress signal had been transmitted, and no one had seen the *Morrell* on radar. At this very moment Charlie Fosbender was still alive, lying next to Dennis Hale. Both men were clinging to life on the raft, hoping to be rescued. Art Stojek and Jack Cleary had died earlier.

Since 9:00 A.M. was the time that the captains were required to report in, Chief Dispatcher Art Dobson was awaiting a call from Captain Crawley. Dobson was manning his post at Bethlehem Steel's steamship headquarters in Cleveland. But there was no word from the *Morrell's* captain. They had heard from Captain Connelly of the *Townsend,* but the *Morrell* was mysteriously missing.

No one wanted to think the worst. The thought was too horrible to mention. It was best to keep looking and praying for the ship's safety. There was always the hope that she would show up, blown off course and banged up, but nonetheless safe. After all, there was no call for help. But a frightening possibility loomed large, and everyone had to be wondering if the storm had claimed the *Morrell* and her crew.

By two that afternoon, Captain Connelly reported to Bethlehem Steel that he had last contacted the *Morrell* at 12:15 A.M., and he believed she was still about fifteen miles ahead. Dobson contacted the *Arthur B. Homer*, thinking that she would at some point pass the *Morrell*. He advised the captain to be on the lookout. No luck. The *Homer* could not even make radio contact with the ship.

Still not hearing a word from the *Morrell* by evening, Art Dobson at Bethlehem Steel was becoming increasingly concerned. He tried desperately to make radio contact with Captain Crawley. But no one on the lake had seen or heard from the freighter. Again, Dobson told the captains of Bethlehem Steel's two steamships on Lake Huron, the *Townsend* and *Arthur B. Homer*, to continue to attempt radio contact. Maybe the *Morrell* was still sailing but without a functioning radio. Maybe the storm had knocked out her radio antenna. But with each hour that passed, hope for the *Morrell*'s survival slipped away. Bethlehem Steel was getting very worried. It was highly unusual for such a long time to pass with no contact, visual or radio. By the evening of the twenty-ninth, it had been eighteen hours since anyone had heard from the *Morrell*.

Attempting to track down the missing ship, Dobson contacted the Rogers City marine radio station, located at the northern tip of Michigan's Mitten. They said they had heard nothing from or about the *Morrell* on any radio frequency during the storm. By nightfall, there was still no word from the *Morrell*—no one had seen or heard from her. Bethlehem Steel hoped that the morning would bring happier news.

By Wednesday morning at 9:00 A.M., no one could have been surprised when the *Morrell* failed to report in for the second straight day. Increasingly concerned about their ship's safety, Bethlehem Steel repeatedly tried to make contact, but of course it was futile.

Later that morning, while uncertainty swirled around the lakes and speculation crackled over the airwaves, a raft from the *Morrell* was caught up on some rocks just offshore. Dennis Hale, too weak to move, was lying there, surrounded by three corpses. Fosbender had passed away the day before in the late afternoon. Incredibly, Bethlehem Steel had *still* not notified the Coast Guard that the *Morrell* was missing—a day and a half since anyone had spoken with the ship! At this very moment, Hale was calling out for help, but no one heard. It was the story of the *Morrell's* wreck, once again. No one saw and no one knew.

Throughout all of this, the *Townsend* continued her northerly course up Lake Huron. The freighter eventually made her way to the St. Mary's River, preparing to enter the Soo Locks, which would ease the ship into Lake Superior for the final leg of the long journey to Taconite Harbor, Minnesota.

The storm-battered *Townsend* pulled into the Lime Island fueling station on St. Mary's River. Just as a stop at a gas station gives the driver a chance to inspect a car, this fueling gave Captain Connelly an opportunity to inspect his vessel to see if the storm had caused any damage. First and most obviously, he noticed that there were loose rivets in the hull's steel plating in several places, but this was not unusual for the big haulers after enduring rough weather. So many rivets can pop off the plates that bucketsful can be collected at the end of a rough voyage.

Surprisingly, while navigating the storm, Connelly had not been aware of any structural damage even though the ship was stressed and had a tough time holding a course. So Connelly was startled by what he discovered next—a two-foot crack, about an eighth of an inch wide, beginning at the right corner of the number 10 hatch. It was about halfway down the main deck, and that alone was cause for grave concern. The crack was serious enough to have allowed four feet of water into the cargo hold!

The *Townsend* had indeed suffered damage like the *Morrell's*—a tear in the steel occurred suddenly and without warning. The steel plating on these two sister ships had reacted to the same storm in a similar way. But unlike the *Townsend,* the crack in the *Morrell* was severe enough for her to break in two.

The *Townsend's* damage was extremely serious, and Captain Connelly may have wondered if the *Morrell* had developed a more disastrous fracture. To be sure, the *Townsend* and her crew were very lucky on that November night. They would never know how close they came to suffering the same tragic end as the *Morrell.* The *Townsend's* crack was so severe that she never completed the final journey to Minnesota and remained docked at Sault Ste. Marie. In fact, after barely surviving the death storm of 1966, the *Townsend* never sailed again.

Connelly reported his findings to Dobson at the central headquarters in Cleveland, adding that the Coast Guard was going to perform an official inspection of his vessel. Both men must have been thinking the same thing. The *Morrell* was following the same route, only she was twenty miles ahead of the *Townsend*. Based on that information, the *Morrell* should have reached the St. Mary's River, the gateway to Lake Superior, well before the *Townsend*. The last ray of hope had been all but extinguished.

It was at noon, twenty-seven hours after the *Morrell* had failed to send in her first required radio report, when Bethlehem Steel finally informed the Coast Guard Rescue Coordination Center in Cleveland of the missing ship. The Coast Guard put out an alert to all vessels on Lake Huron, a sort of all-points bulletin for the *Morrell*. The search had begun. In retrospect, many have wondered why the Coast Guard had not been notified earlier. Twenty-nine men were missing. Even a missing-person report can be issued after twenty-four hours, and yet no one had heard a word from the *Morrell* for thirty-six hours!

The Coast Guard search-and-rescue operation kicked into high gear. Three Coast Guard cutters were ordered into the search—the *Mackinaw*, *Bramble*, and *Acacia*. These three large and powerful cutters were experienced at forging their way through violent and dangerous seas. Lake Huron was still very rough, and these mighty rescue ships, manned by their able crews, battled the towering waves and howling winds. In addition, four more craft were sent from the Harbor Beach, Port Huron, and Saginaw River Coast Guard stations. Finally, from the Traverse City Coast Guard Air Station, two helicopters and two planes flew to the scene, as did two more helicopters from the Detroit Coast Guard Air Station.

In all, thirteen vessels, small craft, helicopters, and planes participated in the search. The entire operation was coordinated by the impressive *Mackinaw*, the world's most powerful icebreaker. At a muscular 290 feet, the football-shaped *Mack*, skippered by Captain George D. Winstein, was the largest Coast Guard cutter to ever sail the Great Lakes. Despite the all-out air and sea effort, Captain Winstein did not hold out much hope for any survivors under these adverse conditions. It was all much too late. The ship had perished thirty-four hours ago.

By this time the news media had heard of the missing ship and began reporting whatever information they could gather, regardless of how inaccurate it was. The *Buffalo Courier-Express* headline on December 1, 1966 read "Lakes Freighter Sinks; 32 Crewmen Lose Lives." Similarly, on the same day, newspaper headlines from Washington, D.C., to Chicago mistakenly reported thirty-two crewmen lost. It seems that even the twenty-nine-man crew aboard the *Morrell* was a mystery.

Shortly after noon, just ten minutes after the Coast Guard began its search, the freighter *C.G. Post* spotted a body floating eight miles off of Harbor Beach. He was wearing a *Daniel J. Morrell* life jacket and was the first casualty sighted. Sadly, there would be many more.

CHAPTER ELEVEN

"WAITING TO DIE"

O n the evening of November 29, the day before the Coast Guard began its search, one man was still miraculously alive—but just barely. Frostbitten on his feet and hands, exhausted, and nearly starving, the once robust Hale had now lost nearly twenty-five pounds and was too weak to move. Clinging to life, he was adrift with the bodies of his three shipmates. His friend Fuzzy had died just a few hours before, and darkness was once again closing in. But since late afternoon, when he died, the raft had been drifting, ever so slowly, closer to shore. Fuzzy must have been right when he said there was land off in the distance.

Suddenly, the raft stopped. Although he was semiconscious, Hale knew that he had landed on an outcropping of boulders, only a couple hundred feet from shore. He was so close that his blurry eyes could see the friendly twinkle of lights in the windows of a tiny farmhouse. But he was too weak to move a muscle, let alone walk on his frozen feet. Hale recalled, "I could have waded to shore, but my body was paralyzed with cold and pain."

So he yelled. He yelled as loud as he could and then he yelled some more. But no one heard him. When he thought he saw a boat off in the distance, he managed to launch a flare from the broken flare gun. It was his last flare. Three had been fired early Tuesday morning, shortly after the ship went down, and one was lost overboard. But it did not matter. What he thought was a ship turned out to be just a buoy.

He was tantalizingly close to being rescued but still could not make it to safety. What would it take to be saved? The raft had carried him nearly to shore and still no one saw him! And then things got even worse. The snow began falling on his bare legs, the temperature dropped, and Huron's waves continued to pound the shore and batter the raft against the rocks. Hale had to steel himself to yet another endless night on the raft.

Surrounded by the lonely darkness, amid the blowing snow and chilling wind, Hale could see the long, white beam from Pointe Aux Barques Lighthouse as it slowly panned across the endless expanse of raging sea. Each time the powerful beam's motion swept in his direction, penetrating the blackness, he could see his bare legs and feet illuminated as the raft rocked unevenly against the outcropping of boulders. The twinkling lights of the farmhouse and the lighthouse's blazing shaft of light offered little reassurance. He was alone, surrounded by three corpses. No matter how close he was to land or rescue, no one had seen him. Nobody even knew that he was missing. And worst of all, the long night was just beginning.

When the morning of Wednesday, November 30 finally arrived with its comforting light, Hale once again yelled for help. No one heard him except the seagulls looking for their morning scraps. Eight o'clock in the morning marked thirty hours on the raft. Amazingly, no one was out searching for the lost crew!

By noon, the raft was still grounded between the boulders, and no one had seen or heard him. Ironically, though he was surrounded by water, he had become extremely thirsty and dehydrated. For hours, he had dipped into the water a lanyard, or length of string, attached to the grip of the flare gun, savoring the few precious drops that it provided. But at some point the string was lost in the lake. Unable to move his body, Hale began to eat the ice chips that were forming on the collar of his peacoat.

Feeling himself drift in and out of consciousness, Hale frequently hallucinated, seeing people of his past in a dreamy, surreal world. At one point he believed that he was reunited with his mother, Ruby, who had died when he was born. He said, "I went to her and she hugged me. It was such a happy feeling."

Then another visitor appeared to him as a white-haired, old man whom he did not recognize. Wearing a long white robe, the old man warned him that no matter how thirsty he became, he must not eat the ice on his coat. Moved by what he had just witnessed, Hale stopped eating the ice.

Later, overcome by thirst, he once again picked at the pieces of ice on his coat. The ghostly apparition reappeared and cast his solemn, deep-set eyes upon him. Slowly shaking a finger at him, the old man told him that the ice would lower his body temperature even more and eventually kill him. The warning was accurate. Because of his weakened condition, eating ice would have been very dangerous. After his second encounter with the mysterious visitor, Hale took no more ice.

Though Hale did not know it, at about noon the Coast Guard had just begun its search. After more than thirty-four hours without food, and at the limits of physical exhaustion, he was aware of very little. All of the energy he had left was put into breathing, staying alive, and praying for help. Slipping in and out of consciousness, he had only his thoughts for company.

By four in the afternoon on November 30, it had been a remarkable thirty-eight hours since Hale's icy immersion into Lake Huron. Sometimes, because of his hallucinations and lapses of consciousness, he was not sure of what he heard or saw. When he heard what sounded like a flock of seagulls flapping their wings high above him and coming closer, he had no idea what was about to happen. Those flapping sounds were not seagulls at all. It was a Coast Guard helicopter! Its crew saw the bright red raft bobbing with the current against some rocks close to the shoreline, about fifteen miles north of Harbor Beach, near the Pointe Aux Barques Lighthouse. The Coast Guard crewmen counted four bodies, all presumed dead. Imagine their surprise and elation when, while hovering above the raft, they saw one man feebly raise his head and with one arm, reach up to them. Dennis Hale had come as close to death as one could. But he was alive, very much alive!

A semiconscious Hale was helped from the raft and transported by helicopter to a hospital in the tiny town of Harbor Beach. Hale could not move while on the raft, and if he had tried, he would have ripped the skin off his leg. His bare feet were totally frostbitten and without feeling. The first words to his rescuers were "I love ya!" He said it over and over. After days adrift and sharing a raft with three lifeless bodies, he needed someone to talk to him. He needed to feel the human touch. He needed to reconnect with the living. Dennis Hale's horrific nightmare, his nineteen-mile journey, had finally come to an end.

The world marveled at how this one man could endure such hardship, surviving one of the most terrible onslaughts of nature. Coast Guardsmen, sailors, doctors, and nurses were in awe of this living miracle who would soon recount his thirty-eight-hour nightmare. One of the rescue pilots, Lieutenant Ward Lewis of Phoenix, Arizona, in awe of this remarkable feat of human endurance, simply said, "I wouldn't think a guy could survive more than two hours in that cold water." Captain George Winstein, skipper of the mighty *Mackinaw*, agreed: "I doubt whether anyone could survive more than three hours at those water temperatures."

When Hale was admitted to the little hospital in Harbor Beach, his body was blue. Having had no experience treating such a severe case of hypothermia, the staff consulted by phone with doctors at the Henry Ford Hospital in Detroit. They were advised that when the body temperature dropped to ninety-four degrees, attempts at warming too rapidly could lead to deadly blood clots. The hospital's attending physician, Dr. Robert Oakes, found that Hale's body temperature was already below that threshold and showing the signs of severe hypothermia. The doctor claimed that Hale's survival was simply a miracle. He had lost twenty-five pounds in thirty-eight hours. In fact, his extra weight may have actually insulated him, protecting him from the cold. Ironically, not having shoes or pants may have also been an advantage, for they could have frozen to him, lowering his body temperature further and plunging him into

At an impressive 220 feet, the *Mackinaw* was the Coast Guard's largest cutter and a major player in the *Morrell* search. Courtesy of Jack Deo, Superior View Photography.

In 1906 the *Daniel J. Morrell* was launched under ominously dark skies. Courtesy of the Dossin Great Lakes Museum and the Detroit Historical Society.

An underwater image of the *Morrell's* steam whistle, which was attached to the ship's smokestack on the stern section. Courtesy of the Dossin Great Lakes Museum and the Detroit Historical Society.

The *Edward Y. Townsend* cutting a path through choppy waters. Courtesy of the Dossin Great Lakes Museum and the Detroit Historical Society.

The 603-foot *Morrell* was an impressive presence on the lakes. Courtesy of Historical Collections of the Great Lakes, Bowling Green State University.

The *Morrell* coming up on Little Rapids Cut at Sault Ste. Marie. The black smokestack shows that this picture was taken before 1927, when the *Morrell* was still managed by the Hanna Company. Courtesy of Historical Collections of the Great Lakes, Bowling Green State University.

A view of the *Morrell's* stern. It's a long way from one end to the other! Courtesy of Historical Collections of the Great Lakes, Bowling Green State University.

A crowd gathered to watch the launching of the *Townsend* in 1906, the same year the *Morrell* was launched. Courtesy of Historical Collections of the Great Lakes, Bowling Green State University.

Standing near the place where he was rescued, survivor Dennis Hale holds a wooden shard from one of the *Morrell*'s lifeboats. Courtesy of Dennis Hale.

Wheelsman Charles "Fuzzy" Fosbender shared the raft with Dennis Hale, Art Stojek, and Jack Cleary. Courtesy of *Port Huron Times Herald.*

Dennis Hale (right) and shipmate Sam Grippi shown here during happier times. Courtesy of Dennis Hale.

The Coast Guard rescue of Dennis Hale. Photograph by *Times Herald* photographer Ralph Polovich, courtesy of *Port Huron Times Herald.*

A grateful but barely conscious Dennis Hale was taken from the helicopter to a waiting ambulance and transported to the Harbor Beach hospital. Courtesy of *Port Huron Times Herald.*

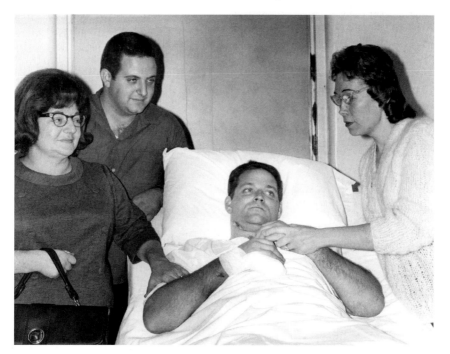

Dennis Hale, in his hospital bed, is surrounded (*left to right*) by his stepmother Cecelia, his brother Louis, and his wife Bertha. Courtesy of *Port Huron Times Herald*.

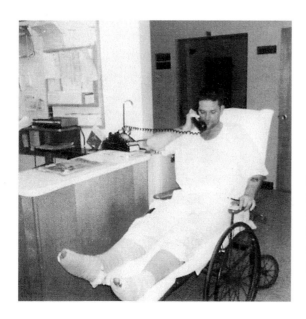

Still hospitalized after his harrowing ordeal, Dennis Hale, with heavily bandaged feet, makes a call from his wheelchair. Courtesy of Dennis Hale.

Young Jack Cleary, shown here in his Navy uniform, made it to the raft but did not survive. Courtesy of Sandy Cleary Peer.

Dennis Hale's lifejacket. Courtesy of Dennis Hale.

A life-raft identical to the one Hale survived on for thirty-eight hours. Courtesy of S.S. *Valley Camp.*

a fatal hypothermia. In addition, somehow he was able to get about two hours of sleep while on the raft. All of this, combined with his youth, a husky build, and a lot of luck, helped him survive.

The next day from his hospital bed, Hale revealed, "I was in such pain, I was hoping to die. I had given up hope. I was just waiting to die."

CHAPTER TWELVE

AND THE BODIES KEEP COMING

lthough the *Morrell* disappeared in the early morning darkness during a blizzard on Tuesday, November 29, the first victim was not spotted for thirty-four hours. Shortly after noon on the next day, the crew of the *C.G. Post* saw a body floating eight miles off of Harbor Beach. The freighter reported her discovery to the Harbor Beach Coast Guard Station, which immediately dispatched a boat to recover it. Four hours later, seven more bodies were recovered, bringing the total to eight. Rescue pilot Lieutenant Ward Lewis reported back from the search with the ominous words, "That water was terrible. It was cold and full of death." He later added that most of the bodies were seen "together in clusters, about five miles off shore."

The first bodies to be recovered were positively identified as Captain Arthur Crawley, First Mate Phillip Kapets, Second Mate Duncan MacLeod, Wheelsman Henry Rischmiller, Wheelsman Stuart Campbell, Watchman Albert Whoeme, Watchman Norman Bragg, and Ordinary Deckwatch Larry Davis.

While the lifeless bodies were being dragged out of the lake, something else was happening—something that no one could have predicted or even believed. It was four o'clock that afternoon when Dennis Hale was seen just barely alive on a raft, surrounded by the three corpses of Art Stojek, Jack Cleary, and Fuzzy Fosbender. These three men raised the death toll to eleven. Sadly, the magnitude of this tragedy was just beginning to unfold. The bodies would keep coming.

The next day was a grisly continuation of the day before, and one that many families would never forget. It started off at nine-thirty in the morning with the recovery of the body of another crewman. Fifteen minutes later, two more were picked up by the Coast Guard cutter *Acacia*. This was the rescue boat that was in the vicinity of the *Morrell*, battling the same rough seas during the early morning hours of November 29. But unlike the doomed *Morrell*, the *Acacia* reversed her course at three o'clock in the morning (one hour after the *Morrell* broke up), seeking the safe shelter of Port Huron.

Searching for more bodies and hoping that Hale would not be the only survivor, the Coast Guard's search and rescue was in full force. The cutters *Mackinaw*, *Bramble*, and *Acacia* braved blizzard conditions in the teeth of 45 mph winds as they performed their search. Together the three ships ran a crisscross course that covered an area of four hundred square miles and extended from Harbor Beach on the northeastern coast of Michigan's Thumb, northward to Pointe Aux Barques. The blinding snow and fierce winds reduced visibility to just a half mile. Even so, a dedicated one-hundred-member search party on land endured freezing temperatures as they walked up and down the shoreline, looking for any sign of the *Morrell*'s crew.

By two o'clock the *Acacia* had pulled six more bodies from the angry waters. A horrifying total of nine bodies were found that day: Chief Engineer John Schmidt, First Assistant Engineer Valmour Marchildon, Second Cook Nicholas Homick, Porter Joseph Mahsen, Porter Charles Sestakauskas, Fireman Arthur Fargo, Fireman Chester Konieczka, Oiler Wilson Simpson, and Coalpasser Leon Truman. Many were only partially clothed since most had been awakened from their sleep when the ship began to tear apart. The bodies were taken to a funeral home in Harbor Beach, where they were later identified by FBI fingerprint experts. Twenty members of the lost crew had been recovered and identified as dead by drowning or exposure. Only one was still alive. Eight crewmen were still missing and presumed dead.

By this time, however, yet another body had been seen and reported. But through a strange and puzzling series of events, it was neither identified nor recovered for many days. It all began at 2:45 on Wednesday afternoon, just an hour before Dennis Hale's raft was spotted. Earl Gudakunst of Huron City, on the northern Thumb, was standing on the shore by his home on Lake Huron when he saw something suspicious. It looked like a life raft stuck on a reef about a half mile away. He and a friend, Ken Schave, set off in Earl's small boat to see what the object was.

The seas were rough and the winds were blowing the little boat around as they struggled out to the reef. As he approached, Gudakunst indeed discovered a life raft. And she was from the *Morrell*'s stern! What he saw then he would remember his whole life. It was a man's foot just beneath the water's surface, sticking out from under the raft. The two men boarded the raft, leaned over her edge, grabbed the ankle, and pulled the leg out of the water. At that moment the men were horrified by what they saw. The life-jacketed corpse of a crewman from the *Morrell* had become grotesquely wedged between the oil-drum pontoons. Afraid that the unidentified body would be washed away, they secured the body to the raft with about five feet of rope.

Gudakunst did not know this, but during an earlier air search, Coast Guard helicopter pilots had already located the raft, but their search did not reveal what was underneath. Consequently, the raft was of no immediate concern. Gudakunst and Schave hurried back to shore in their little duck boat to report their discovery. As soon as they landed, Gudakunst reported his finding to the sheriff, who relayed the message to the Coast Guard. But things were hectic. After all, this was about the time Dennis Hale was being rescued on another raft.

After reporting the body, Gudakunst believed that someone would soon arrive to bring it to the morgue and identify it, but he was mistaken. Much to his surprise and disappointment, no effort was made to recover the mystery body until the following Monday. For five days the crewman's corpse remained bound to the raft without any attempt at recovery or identification. Each day, a frustrated Gudakunst looked out of his window and saw the undisturbed raft buoying up and down. How upsetting it was for him to know that a dead body was floating just beyond his property—for days. The unidentified man's family believed their loved one had not yet been found. Each day must have been horrible as they awaited any word from the authorities. In all, they endured a five-day wait, long after most of the other bodies of the *Morrell*'s crew had been recovered, before they would hear of the offshore corpse.

Finally, at eight-thirty on the evening of Monday, December 5, the body of thirty-eight-year-old George Dahl, the *Morrell*'s third assistant engineer, was retrieved and identified. Dahl was a married man who made his home in Duluth, Minnesota, on Lake Superior. He became the twenty-first crewman to be found and identified.

When the story of the mystery sailor became public, speculation began to abound. How did this man come to be wedged between the raft's pontoons? After the *Morrell*'s bow slipped beneath the surface, the stern continued to plow southward on her lonely path into the darkness. But she was not empty. Considering the time of night that the *Morrell* broke up, there may have been as many as seventeen men aboard the stern. Were they able to launch the stern's raft? Were Dahl and other passengers on that raft? Probably not. According to Lieutenant Lewis, "One man had died apparently because he got stuck under the raft. . . . Apparently, when the boat started to sink, they dropped the raft over this guy, and his head got stuck between the drums."

In addition to locating the two life rafts and the gruesome task of recovering the bodies, the Coast Guard found remnants and debris from the *Morrell,* including life jackets, life rings, and boat oars.

After George Dahl was identified on Monday evening, there were no more reports of bodies until the next weekend. At around noon on Saturday, December 10, a ten-year-old boy found the body of Saverio Grippi, a fifty-three-year-old coalpasser, washed ashore on the beach at Tiverton, Ontario. Grippi's body was fully clothed, and he was wearing a life jacket from the *Morrell.* In the two weeks since the sinking, Grippi's body had been carried clear across Lake Huron to the Canadian province of Ontario.

The loss of "Sam," as the crew called him, hit Dennis Hale hard. They had been good friends, and when they were not working on the big boats, they liked to go rabbit hunting together. Both were from the Lake Erie port town of Ashtabula, and on more than one occasion, Sam and his wife, Sarah, had invited Dennis, Bertha, and the kids over for spaghetti dinners.

Sam Grippi was the last crewman found before the spring thaw. By the year's end, twenty-two bodies had been identified. Thirteen had drowned and nine died of exposure. Dennis Hale was the only man who could offer an eyewitness account of the terror of that night.

As winter loosened its icy grip on the Great Lakes, the gentle breezes of spring were welcomed back, for they signaled new life. Families of those affected by the *Morrell* disaster were trying to move forward with their lives. But the tragedy seemed to have no end. On Saturday, April 15, many months after the freighter sank, yet another gruesome discovery was made on Lake Huron's Canadian shore. The body of Oiler Don Worcester had washed ashore on Chantry Island, about two miles from Southhampton, Ontario. Worcester was thirty-eight years old and the father of four children. How difficult life must have been for his wife and children. Back at home in Maine, Worcester's family had endured a painful Christmas, not knowing anything about their husband and father. All winter long they waited for word, but never knew his fate until this moment.

The next day, Sunday, another body was found in the same area. But unlike Worcester, this body was too decomposed to be identified. The thumb and fingerprints were almost totally gone and required three weeks of FBI restoration, treating the fingers so that an identification could be made. Finally, the man was identified as Third Mate Ernie Marcotte.

These men were two of the last faces that Dennis Hale remembers seeing while crouched on that raft with the other crew, waiting for their sudden immersion into the lake's turbulent waters. Worcester was standing on the stern, holding his oil can, staring blankly at the stormy sea. Hale saw Marcotte just below the pilothouse and well above the deck, as if he were calmly awaiting his fate. For nearly five months, the bodies drifted unnoticed and untouched, seventy miles from where the *Morrell* sank, all the way to Lake Huron's distant shore.

And the bodies still kept coming. On May 20, teenager David Price was found on the shore of the Bruce Peninsula, also on the Canadian side of Lake Huron. At nineteen, Price, a coalpasser, was the *Morrell's* youngest crewman. His was the twenty-fifth body recovered. And six months after the wreck, May 27, 1967, the badly decomposed body of Alfred Norkunas washed ashore, wearing only shoes. Norkunas, of Superior, Wisconsin, was found seven miles east of Port Austin on the tip of the Thumb. Because of the body's advanced decomposition, the FBI in Washington, D.C., was needed to positively identify it. Norkunas was the *Morrell's* second assistant engineer and was thirty-nine. His was the twenty-sixth and last body to be recovered.

By June, there were still two men missing, According to all available records, Steward Stanley Satlawa and Deckhand John Groh were never found. Satlawa was forty years old and came from Buffalo. Groh was the twenty-one-year-old who rode with his friend Dennis Hale for a quick visit home to his family in Erie, while Hale continued on to his home in Ashtabula. Although the two deckhands had just missed their ship's departure, they had patiently waited to meet up with the *Morrell* when she reached Windsor, Ontario. When the *Morrell* broke in two, Groh and Hale had both boarded the raft while she was still on the *Morrell's* deck. But that is where their fates diverged. Hale survived. Groh was never again seen.

All that was left were the families, the fathers and mothers, wives and children, sisters and brothers. It was a human wreckage of loss and emptiness.

■ CHAPTER THIRTEEN

HUMAN WRECKAGE

Immediately visible after a shipwreck is the scattered debris that drifts
and floats aimlessly, bobbing with the rhythm of the waves, sometimes
for days. The life jackets, life rings, fragments of wood and shards of
metal, perhaps a disengaged lifeboat oar are all remnants of an earlier
violence. But terrible tragedies leave something else behind—an emptiness
of the heart. It is the human wreckage of the directionless, lost souls of
those who must somehow cope with the immeasurable pain of losing a
husband, son, father, or brother.

These are the forgotten victims of the *Morrell*. What answers can be
given to their penetrating questions? How do you explain to them that the
ship simply broke in two? Could something more have been done to save
the ship and her crew? Why did it take so long to report the ship missing?
Why was there just one survivor? And if one could survive, why not more?

What words can ease their pain? The questions flowed faster and more
bitterly than any answers. The pain of living became more unbearable,
more palpable than anything they had ever endured. It was a type of
suffering that you cannot explain to others, like losing someone in a
war. Perhaps it was the suddenness of the loss that made this tragedy so
tangible, so physically painful. These men were ripped away from their

families just as unexpectedly and violently as the *Morrell* herself had been torn in two. One day the families were praying for a safe return from the final voyage and sharing the holiday celebrations. Next, word comes that they are gone. So simple and cold.

On Monday, December 5, Dennis Hale was released from the little hospital in Harbor Beach. Viewed by nurses, doctors, seamen, the press, and the public in general as a miracle man, Hale could not have been prepared for the emotional storm that lay ahead. He was alive, and that was enough for now. Accompanied by his wife Bertha, his older brother, Louis, and his stepmother Cecelia, Dennis looked forward to being reunited with his four children. But would he ever be able to return to a normal life? The years ahead would reveal the answer.

The next day, services for the twenty-eight men who perished a week earlier were held at Our Lady of Lake Huron Catholic Church. Unlike Hale, none of his twenty-eight shipmates would be going home. The church was packed with Catholic, Presbyterian, and Baptist mourners. Throughout the service, everyone prayed for those lost. Many of the mourners did not even know the men. Referring to the doomed crew, one minister observed, "We did not know them, but we are strangely touched by their passing." Another clergyman expressed sympathy for those who were left to pick up the pieces of their lives: "Our hearts cry with the families for the loss of their loved ones." The truth had become known, the ship went down, and twenty-eight men would no longer walk with their families. The pain had been unleashed, and the long grieving process had begun.

For the rest of the world, life went on. The *Morrell* was no longer front-page news, and, as is often the case following a great human tragedy, people quickly turned their attention to other things. The country was embroiled in the Vietnam War, anti-war protests exploded on college campuses, and President Lyndon Johnson's popularity was steadily declining over the unpopular war. Just a couple of days after the *Morrell* sank, the tragedy was all but forgotten. Twenty-eight men had died, and their memory would only live on in their families and friends. But what about the loved ones who continued in the face of the worst loss imaginable? How could they go on?

By daybreak on Tuesday, November 29, Jack Cleary was lying dead alongside his shipmates on a raft in the middle of Lake Huron. And no one even knew the *Morrell* had sunk. That evening, unaware of the deadly events that had taken place, the Cleary household in Cleveland was busy decorating and preparing for a birthday celebration. Jack's little sister, Sandy, was going to turn ten the next day. Sandy, the youngest of the four Cleary children, was ten years younger than Jack, who was the eldest.

The next day, Wednesday, was of course a school day for Sandy, but later she had a wonderful birthday party, enjoying lots of cake, ice cream, games, and presents. It was a joyous occasion for everyone. She went to bed that night with a happy feeling. It had been a good day—up to that point. But later that night, Sandy's parents received a horrible phone call. A raft had been found late that afternoon, and the Coast Guard thought that it would be a good idea for John, Sr. to drive up to Harbor Beach and identify a body that they suspected was his son. The one glimmer of hope, was that the body was not Jack's because he may not have even been aboard the freighter. A couple of days earlier they had heard that Jack had called his girlfriend and told her he was getting off the *Morrell* at Detroit. If that were true, then all of this was just a cruel mistake.

Sandy knew nothing of this until she was awakened by her mother the next morning, Thursday, December 1. After blinking her sleepy eyes open, Sandy's first words to her mother were that she didn't feel so good. Perhaps she had eaten too much cake the night before, and she just did not feel well enough to go to school. Her mom was very understanding and said that she agreed. It was not a good day to go to school. It was then that she said to Sandy, "We think your brother got killed." The shock that ran through her body at that moment cannot be imagined. Things were so good last night. Everyone was happy. Jack *had* to be coming home. Her mother's very words "we *think*" preserved the slightest germ of hope. It meant they were not absolutely sure. And if they were not sure, then he might still be alive.

But all of this anguishing over words and their meanings proved futile and pointless. Jack was dead, and that was certain. From that day on, Sandy's birthday would be forever linked to the heart-wrenching memory of the loss of her big brother. It would be forty years before Sandy would permit herself to celebrate her birthday again.

In another household, on November 30, Jan Fosbender was in her home on Royal Street in St. Clair, Michigan, thumbing through the day's mail. Among the letters, Jan found one from her husband and sat down to read it. It was comforting, almost as if he were right there beside her, talking to her. Although it was the day after the horrible end, the families had no knowledge of the missing ship or her crew until the first life-jacketed body was found at about noon. With Dennis Hale beside him, Charlie had survived fourteen grueling hours on the life raft. But Jan had no way of knowing that late in the afternoon on the previous day, her husband had passed away. And most heartbreaking of all, before dying he had seen the raft slowly drawn toward the shore. Yet it would be a full twenty-four hours before the raft would be discovered.

Waiting for any news about the *Morrell*'s crew, Jan sat with neighbors in her kitchen, tuned in to a local radio station. Her friends kept her company throughout the painful ordeal, knowing how much she needed their support. Over and over she read Charlie's letter, especially one line: "If our luck holds with us, it will be our last trip." His hopeful words betrayed a hint of uncertainty.

Jan and Charlie had only been married for four years, and Jan had two grown children from a previous marriage. It was the forty-two-year-old wheelsman's first marriage. In fact, their fourth anniversary had been about three weeks ago, on November 10, but they had not seen each other for a month. Life aboard the freighters meant being away from home for long periods of time. Consequently, the wives of these sailors were strong, independent women who were charged with managing the entire household.

Surrounded by her friends, Jan's painful waiting dragged on until late afternoon. Everyone was quietly visiting when suddenly a hush came over the room. The radio announcer excitedly reported that a survivor on a raft had been rescued. Knowing that it was just one survivor, Charlie's wife said, "I still got my hopes up," so she continued to wait and pray.

Eventually, she learned that the one survivor had shared the raft with her Charlie. The same Charlie who, as just a young kid, survived despite being placed in harm's way as an Air Force tailgunner in Europe during World War II. But this November death storm was a bullet that he would not be able to dodge. On Saturday night, Charlie had spoken his final words to his wife by telephone before setting sail from Buffalo. Those words proved eerily prophetic. Jan recalled that "he said it would be his last trip of the season."

On the afternoon of November 30, Cecilia Stojek was cleaning up the dishes from lunch in the kitchen of her home in Buffalo. Her four kids were outside playing, and she was listening to the radio, perhaps daydreaming about when her husband Art would be home again. Things would be good. She had celebrated her birthday on November 12, a little more than two weeks before, and although times were tough and money was tight, she knew they would be able to make things work out. Suddenly, the radio announced a special report about a ship that had disappeared in Lake Huron. She was the *Daniel J. Morrell!* Cecilia dropped the dish she was holding. No, it could not be true. Is Art alive? Are there any survivors? Where is Art? Her head swirled with terror as she collapsed to the floor. The radio—that's how Cecilia Stojek found out about the wreck of the *Morrell.*

For some, the pain of loss was simply too much to bear. The death of Leon Truman, a coalpasser from Toledo, plunged his wife Jenny into a dark depression. Listless, weak, and unresponsive, Jenny, the mother of two, was hospitalized. In a 1992 videotaped interview, Jenny recalled what life was like without Leon:

> I didn't want nothin' to do with my kids. . . . My two girls—I didn't want nothing to do with them. I wanted to die. I loved him. He was my life. I wanted to die. . . . There's always going to be the memories and

they can't take them away from me. Nobody can take memories away from somebody. . . . I just feel bad for the other people that had to go through the same thing.

During the same interview, Jenny's daughter, Darlene, who was four years old at the time, recalled visiting her mom in the hospital one day and witnessing a turning point in her recovery:

I remember going to the hospital and . . . hearing the boats go by on the river. And she was just laying there, just kind of staring off into space. It seemed like she didn't recognize us or anything. . . . And I remember looking down at her and saying, "I love you, Mommy. I love you. I love you. Please love me back. Please come home."

These sweet, heartfelt words from her four-year-old daughter were enough to rescue Jenny from her overwhelming grief and sadness. At that point Jenny finally felt something the doctors and medicines could not provide—a reason for going on with life.

As the weeks and months passed, the families wanted answers from Bethlehem Steel. The company said that they had tried unsuccessfully to contact the *Morrell* all day on Tuesday, November 29. By Thursday, December 1, the Port Huron *Times Herald* was already asking company officials, in Bethlehem, Pennsylvania, "Why was it some 36 hours from the time the ship was last contacted Tuesday (midnight) until a body was found Wednesday, that no communication was received from the *Morrell* or there was no alarm put out that she was missing?" The company's position was that "all day Tuesday, through our Cleveland office, we tried to contact the ship. But it was reported to us that vessels were arriving at the head of Lake Huron with their masts and antennae ice-covered or broken, which of course would affect radio communications."

After no communication from the *Morrell* all day Tuesday, Bethlehem Steel finally took more decisive action. A spokesperson for the company explained, "On Wednesday morning, when the *Morrell* did not report at Detour, Michigan, we contacted the Coast Guard, which issued an all-ships alert." The Coast Guard said that the Cleveland office of Bethlehem Steel contacted them at the time the first body from the *Morrell* was spotted by the freighter *C.G. Post.*

Despite grave concerns for her whereabouts, no search had begun for the doomed ship until a full day and a half after the *Morrell's* last radio transmission. The answers were unsatisfactory and the families were not impressed. They needed closure.

CHAPTER FOURTEEN

SEEKING ANSWERS

O ver the months that followed the tragedy, the families' grief began to express itself as anger and frustration. They wanted to know whether the *Daniel J. Morrell* was actually seaworthy at the time of her demise. How could she be torn in two pieces, just like the *Carl D. Bradley* on another stormy November night, eight years earlier on Lake Michigan? The loss of the *Bradley* in 1958 claimed the lives of thirty-three men, and the sinking of the *Morrell* abruptly ended the lives of twenty-eight men. Sixty-one sailors died in two maritime disasters less than a decade apart and both were eerily similar. Giant vessels the length of two football fields were unceremoniously ripped in half.

Were the stress and pounding of the treacherous seas entirely responsible for the tragedies? Or were the ships themselves in part to blame? Were both the *Morrell* and *Bradley* structurally flawed? Were they like ticking time bombs, about to explode when the unmerciful combination of high winds, powerful waves, cold temperatures, and stress on the hull conspired to take them down? The families needed answers, not excuses. They needed to know if Bethlehem Steel was in some way responsible and if this tragedy could have been avoided. And they wanted to know what could be done to prevent future nightmares for the families of those who depend on the freighters for their livelihood.

It was amid this tempest of concern, controversy, and a quest for answers that the U.S. Coast Guard Marine Board began its hearings on December 5, beginning an investigation that lasted until March. Lawsuits were filed on behalf of those who perished, and people wanted to know the truth of what exactly happened on that terrible night and the days that immediately followed.

A PARADE OF TESTIMONY

Retracing the events in the months leading up to the final journey, it was noted that during the off-season, back in February 1966, the *Morrell* had been given a thorough going over by seven inspectors while she was in dry dock in Toledo. No major problems or need for repairs were observed by the inspectors, just routine things. Then on April 15, the *Morrell* underwent her season-opening annual inspection in Toledo, and again passed muster. On July 20, just four months before the tragedy, it was time for her midseason inspection in Buffalo, and once again she checked out fine. In fact, fire drills and safety drills involving the crew and the lifeboats all met the required standards. By all accounts, the *Morrell* was in good operating condition throughout the 1966 season.

About one week after the *Morrell* was lost at sea, the Coast Guard investigators heard a parade of testimony from company officials and shipping officers. One of the first to testify was Lynn Harivel, fleet engineer for Bethlehem Steel's eight ships. He reported that "there was nothing wrong" with the *Morrell*. However, he acknowledged that when the *Morrell* lost power, there was no emergency battery backup that could be used to send out an SOS. Judging from the men's shifts and posts, Harivel estimated that at the time of the wreck (two o'clock in the morning), there were a dozen men forward and seventeen men riding aboard the stern.

Then, William Hull, the *Morrell*'s captain until Crawley took the helm in August, testified that to the best of his knowledge the ship was in good shape when he left her. In fact, in 1958, when Hull was second mate on the *Morrell,* the ship had handled a November storm on Superior with 100 mph winds and twenty-five-foot seas. It was the same storm that sank the *Bradley* on Lake Michigan. Thomas Burns, the *Morrell's* former third mate who also left the vessel in August, agreed with Hull that the ship was in good condition at that time.

Captain Connelly of the *Townsend* was then summoned before the Board. His testimony focused on the weather the night of the wreck. He claimed that forecasts from the Canadian and American weather services did not accurately reflect the severity of the storm. According to Connelly, in his last communication with the *Morrell,* a little past midnight, Captain Crawley had said that he was struggling to keep the strong winds from blowing his ship sideways. Connelly added that it was the worst storm he had ever witnessed in his twenty-seven-year career on the lakes.

Several other captains were asked to testify, including James Van Buskirk of the *Benson Ford,* Zernie Newman of the *Kinsman Independent,* and Charles Finch of the *Robert Hobson.* All were in the vicinity of the *Morrell* when she met her tragic end. Like Connelly, the captains discussed the inaccurate weather forecasts and insufficient warnings. The seas were so rough, they said, that a lifeboat could not be launched. And, although the *Morrell* and *Townsend* had attempted to forge ahead in the teeth of the gale, some captains had to reverse their northerly course or risk losing their vessel and crew. Their stories revealed a chilling tale of terror in life-threatening seas.

On Friday, December 23, Dennis Hale testified before the Board from his hospital bed at the Ashtabula General Hospital. The Coast Guard officers gathered around his bedside and listened intently as Hale described hearing from two former crew-members of the *Morrell* that there was a problem with leaky rivets that needed replacement—over 1,000 rivets. The Board, however, noted that company officials, inspectors, and surveyors challenged this claim. In fact, Captain Hull, the *Morrell's* former skipper, argued that nowhere near that many rivets needed replacement. He testified that the ship had only about a dozen leaking rivets, and they were repaired by the start of the 1966 season. Nevertheless, Hale stood firm, stating, "If I'd known at the beginning of the season what I found out a week ago . . . I don't think I'd have gone aboard," adding that the ship "was leaking like a sieve."

A SILENT TESTIMONY

The Coast Guard performed a heavy-weather inspection on the *Townsend*, which was anchored at Sault Ste. Marie, after barely escaping the great November storm. While Captain Connelly and his crew waited to be cleared for departure for the final leg of their journey across Lake Superior, he found a two-foot-long structural crack close to the tenth hatch. Consequently, the *Townsend* did not pass her Coast Guard inspection and was not allowed to set sail for the Minnesota shore. Instead, she was towed to a dry dock for repair and more detailed inspection. The *Townsend* would never sail again.

But the implications of this damage went well beyond the *Townsend*. Since the fracture was in the same area of the hull as the crack that led to the destruction of the *Morrell*, it shed some light on why the *Morrell* broke in two. The location of the crack on the *Townsend* (tenth hatch) suggested a structural weakness in the same area as the *Morrell* (eleventh hatch). Combine this with the fact that they were sister ships, built in 1906, and were navigating identical waters. Add to this that the *Carl D. Bradley*'s tragic separation also occurred at the tenth hatch, and the investigators were led to ask why.

The Board concluded that, under certain conditions, the steel used in these older ships could become brittle and split open when exposed to the cold and excessive stress of a classic November gale. If the steel of the *Townsend*, the *Morrell*, or for that matter, the *Bradley*, had been reinforced, perhaps these vessels could have better withstood the incredible stress they had to endure during the storms of November.

If the *Townsend*'s crack had extended itself, the ship could have easily ripped in two, leaving yet another wreck on Lake Huron's murky bottom. But her captain and crew were luckier than the ill-fated crew of the *Morrell*. The *Townsend*'s damage was silent testimony to a structural problem that was shared by both ships, leading investigators to a better understanding of what caused the wreck of the *Daniel J. Morrell*.

THE VERDICT

Four months after the loss of the *Morrell*, the U.S. government formed the National Transportation Safety Board (NTSB). It was (and still is) responsible for investigating the cause of transportation accidents in our country. On February 8, 1968, a five-member board issued a report in response to the Coast Guard's assessment of the causes of the *Morrell* incident. The Coast Guard and the NTSB agreed that the *Morrell* broke up because of structural failure amidships (the ship's middle). The fracture occurred because of the hull's brittleness under the extreme stress of cold temperatures combined with the force of high waves.

Captain Crawley was cleared of blame. There was no way that he or Captain Connelly of the *Townsend* could have known how strong or weak their ships' hulls were, especially under the extreme conditions they were experiencing. While Captain Crawley could judge the weather conditions, it was believed unrealistic to expect him to know his ship's ability to handle those conditions, based on the strength of the hull's steel.

In response to the disturbing series of events surrounding the *Morrell* disaster, the investigators agreed that the decks of ships over four hundred feet long and built with steel manufactured before 1948 had to be reinforced. Naturally, older ships were built out of pre-1948 steel and therefore were more susceptible to fracture due to brittleness. The decision that pre-1948 steel was inferior came from research conducted by the Battelle Memorial Institute of Columbus Laboratories in Ohio. Examining metal fragments taken from the *Morrell*'s stern, they observed that the older steel could become brittle. Consequently, the steel on the older ships was seen as inferior because it did not generate enough flex in high seas and cold weather. It is essential that the big bulk carriers have a little "give" or flex as they hold the sea. Without it, their long decks are susceptible to cracks that can lead to a tragic breakup.

Considering the age of the Great Lakes' fleets, this new information on the flawed steel had far-reaching consequences. At that time, the average age of a Great Lakes freighter was forty-five years. And there were plenty of active cargo carriers that were fifty to sixty years old. There was no question about it: The giants of the lakes were indeed aging—and their crews were at serious risk. In the face of the relatively recent breakup of the *Bradley* and now the *Morrell,* the Coast Guard and the NTSB feared another maritime tragedy and wanted to do everything possible to prevent it from happening again.

The investigators agreed that although no distress signal was sent, report of the missing vessel was too late. In fact, it was noted that only badly flawed procedures would allow a ship to be missing for one and a half days before the Coast Guard was informed. Clearly, Bethlehem Steel's daily reporting system needed to be more responsive to situations where ships failed to report.

Several other lifesaving recommendations were also made. For example, if the sailors had been provided with all-weather survival capsules instead of life rafts, surely more lives could have been saved. These capsules could not be capsized, were fully protected from water, and came equipped with a radio and other survival tools. In addition, all-weather survival suits should have been available. Designed to be put on in less than sixty seconds, these suits can protect imperiled seamen for up to thirteen hours in forty-four-degree water—the same water temperature as on that frigid November night. But remember, no one knew about the *Morrell* until thirty-six hours after she was last heard from. So the thirteen-hour survival suit would only have been beneficial if coupled with a more efficient method for reporting ships that were missing.

Finally, the inspectors decided, there was a serious problem with the *Morrell*'s communications system. No distress signal was sent because of the loss of power that occurred when the main deck started to split open. Fleet Engineer Lynn Harivel explained that when the power was lost, there was no emergency battery backup that could have been used to send out an SOS. One can only imagine how things might have been different if the *Morrell* had been able to broadcast her location and the dire circumstances she was facing.

Considering the dangers of sailing these great ships in November, it was even suggested that freighter activity during the late fall be suspended, for this is when the Great Lakes thrash themselves into a blowing frenzy, endangering ships and their crews.

THE SHIP'S BONES REVEALED

In mid-December Bethlehem Steel hired McQueen Marine, a Canadian company, to locate the broken bones of the *Morrell*. However, bad weather prevented any progress. Then, about three weeks later, on January 6, 1967, a navy aircraft with magnetic detection equipment located a huge area of submerged metal 16.25 miles directly north of Pointe Aux Barques, a tiny township at the tip of Michigan's Thumb. They were hopeful that they had found the wreck of the *Morrell*. The Coast Guard hired Ocean Systems of Alexandria, Virginia, to do the underwater photography of the wreck. The effort to locate and photograph the sunken *Morrell* was coordinated by the Coast Guard cutter *Bramble*, skippered by Lieutenant Commander Herman Pinter.

Headed by R. J. Agness, a retired navy commander, Ocean Systems used an underwater closed-circuit television camera to photograph the mysterious wreck. A 50,000-watt mercury-vapor light illuminated the broken hull that rested in Huron's darkest depths. Pictures were sent up to the *Bramble* by a camera that was mounted so that it could be moved up, down, and sideways. When the images materialized, Agness realized that they had found the *Morrell*'s stern, 216 feet below—the ship's crippled half that refused to give up as she plowed her way into the November darkness.

The stern, which was upright and tilting slightly to the left, had settled into extraordinarily deep, thick mud. The mud was so deep it almost entirely covered the stern and came all the way up to the propeller shaft, within six feet of the main deck. A clock was also found on the stern, stopped at 3:28.

The footage also verified a starboard crack occurring at the eleventh hatch and a portside crack between hatches 11 and 12. The wreck was badly contorted indeed. The twisted metal bent against itself, sometimes at 90° angles and as much as 180°. That meant that the steel was actually bent flat against itself, as effortlessly as a piece of paper folded in half. This ship had been through a war.

Diving of the wreck site continued for the rest of the month of January. Five divers who wore old-fashioned helmets, or "hard hats," tried to take still pictures of the stern with handheld cameras, but bad weather, mud, silt, and cold water made progress slow. In fact, each diver could stay under for no more than thirty minutes at a time.

To get these pictures, the light, the camera, and all other equipment were mounted on a platform that was lowered using the *Bramble*'s long boom (like an arm that extends outward), which was typically used to handle extremely heavy buoys. The camera sent images up to the *Bramble*, where they were videotaped using two monitors—one showing the camera transmission and the other recording it. Those on board could view all of this footage as it was happening.

The video footage told a story of desperate men trying to save themselves. The portside lifeboat of the aft section was missing and may have been launched. Very likely the crewmen trapped aboard the doomed half ship had successfully launched her. But this lifeboat saved no lives. The stern's starboard lifeboat, however, was never deployed. She still rested on the blocks, securely locked in place and covered.

Throughout the entire expedition down to the stern, no bodies were seen. And still the *Morrell*'s bow section was nowhere to be found.

THE OTHER HALF

It would be nearly thirteen years after the *Morrell* went down before the location of her bow section was detected. In May 1979 she was pinpointed about five miles east of the sunken stern. This was incontrovertible evidence that the stern had powered herself an amazing five miles after being torn from her forward half!

Two weeks later, Great Lakes divers Dave Trotter and Larry Coplin embarked on a search for her exact resting spot. Throughout his career, Trotter has surveyed over two thousand square miles of Lake Huron's bottom land, locating the bones of lost ships. Using a boat equipped with side-scanning sonar (high frequency sounds for locating objects), Trotter and Coplin found the *Morrell's* bow sitting upright in two hundred feet of water. The ship's radar screen had toppled, and the divers discovered a fracture at the number 9 hatch. They also found a clock, frozen at 1:55, almost exactly the time *the Morrell* was thought to have foundered. Since the stern's clock read 3:28, it is believed that the stern kept on going for about ninety minutes after the bow's disappearance.

Both halves of the great ship, each about three hundred feet long, had finally been located and analyzed. The video images confirmed a violent breakup, just as Dennis Hale had described. The terrifying minutes that led to an unimaginable tearing of steel and gnashing of metal left the giant freighter and her crew helpless and at the mercy of the raging sea. After sixty years of service on the lakes, the *Morrell* was now at rest, her two pieces separated by the endless blue of Lake Huron.

EPILOGUE

Long after the *Morrell's* headlines faded into history, the families continued to suffer. When a disaster strikes, the nightmare does not end for the loved ones who are left behind to deal with the loss, the grief, the terrible emptiness. Those who were most intimately connected to the tragedy feared that their pain would be forgotten, lost in the shadow of other tragedies that captured the public's attention. Now that the initial shock and horror of the *Morrell's* loss had vanished from the newspapers, who would listen to the lone survivor and all of the families? And because their words went unheeded, what future tragedies that could have been averted would be visited upon other families?

"WHY AM I ALIVE?"

Life was always hard for Dennis Hale. He lost his mother, Ruby, at birth and was raised by his Aunt Inez and then by his stepmother, Cecelia. But by the time he was thirteen, he was pretty much on his own, hitchhiking across the country. One thing about Dennis—he was always testing himself. As a little boy, he would snuggle tight in his blanket during the long, northern Ohio nights. Even though it was December, he would open the windows in his bedroom. As the wintry chill swirled around his tiny room, he imagined how he could keep himself warm in the frigid air. Lying in his bed, Dennis tested his endurance and the limits of his discomfort. He discovered that breathing warm air into his covers generated warmth and that he could warm his hands between his legs and his feet by rubbing them together. Even at that young age, Dennis was thinking like a survivor. Perhaps he was preparing himself in some way for the trauma that would confront him years later.

On December 1, while lying in his bed in the hospital at Harbor Beach, Hale wondered how he, of all of the men on board, was the only one to survive the horrors of that ordeal. On this day, he was visited by a priest, Father Cornelius McEachin. Tormented by the death he had seen, he looked up from his bed and asked, "Father, why am I alive?" The priest told him it was because God wanted him to be alive. Hale understood that, but it did not reach the depth of his pain. Hale told the priest that he thought there was another reason for his survival. He believed it was "because God wants me to suffer before I die." This thought would haunt him for many years.

When he left the hospital Hale was hopeful that he could move forward. He and Bertha had four children and all eagerly awaited his return. What a story he could tell! He had survived a nightmare of brutal cold and endured a vicious storm assault. But would he tell his story? Or was it simply too painful to dredge up the suffering?

Discouraged by the newspapers' inability or unwillingness to accurately report the facts, Hale did not speak to the press for many years. He was frustrated by the misrepresentation of his own words. And he hated when it was wrongly reported in several newspapers that he survived on the raft by seeking shelter under the bodies of his friends. It was disrespectful and hurtful.

As a result, Hale became almost a recluse, a loner who refused to speak in public. He continued to search within himself for reasons why he alone survived. He moved from town to town, working as a machinist and tool-and-die maker in Ohio and Kentucky. Looking back on his life, he wrote in his book, *Sole Survivor*, "It seems as though I was always on the run. . . . I was very unsettled, very frightened. I was trying to outrun something."

Tormented by the guilt of being the only survivor, Hale continually asked himself, "Why me? How come I was the one man spared?" But there were no good answers. In 1991, twenty-five years after the incident, Hale confessed something that revealed the burden a survivor carries after witnessing the loss of so many. In a frightening and chilling revelation, Hale said, "If I had it to do all over again I wouldn't go near that raft. I think I would grab the binnacle and go down with the ship. It has been too much to deal with."

Though Dennis Hale's emotional healing was slow in coming, eventually he broke his silence and began to discuss his ordeal publicly. He learned that this gave him some peace and comfort. Yet there are still things about that horrible night and the days that followed that he cannot discuss.

Through the decades following the accident, Hale's daily struggles continued. Married five times and battling bouts of drug abuse, his path to recovery was long and arduous. And effects of the tragedy went beyond psychological torment. After his rescue, Hale was in and out of the hospital repeatedly. Several surgeries were performed on his frostbitten feet and toes—ten operations on his left foot alone, including the amputation of his baby toe.

Despite attempts to overcome the terrible memory, Dennis Hale is still haunted by the physical, psychological, and emotional pain of those thirty-eight hours, recalling the twenty-eight men that perished. To this day he sees faces in the crowd that remind him of men on the *Morrell*. But talking about his ordeal has been good therapy, and Hale believes that every time he reveals his feelings about the incident, he learns something more about himself. In a newspaper interview in 2004 with the *Bay City Times*, thirty-eight years after the disaster, the sixty-four-year-old Hale said, "I really don't know how to die. Life has always been a struggle for me [but] . . . I had the will to survive."

That will to survive has sustained Dennis Hale through the greatest storm of his life—the struggle within himself.

GRIEVING FAMILIES SEEK JUSTICE

In the aftermath of the tragedy, the families began a painful journey. Some had to face their grief alone. Others found support from friends. And some of the surviving families were comforted by each other, those who also lost loved ones on that same night. Lawsuits demanded some measure of accountability from Bethlehem Steel, but money is a poor substitute. It does not heal the emotional wounds and psychological scars.

A human tragedy of this magnitude can awaken an otherwise dormant sense of ethics. Though families suffer unfathomable grief, impersonal corporations do not freely accept blame or responsibility. Sadly, it seems that profit often dictates motive and behavior. Therefore, the victims of tragedy must seek closure in another way. In this case, the families of the crew sought some accountability for the disastrous sequence of events surrounding November 29. Someone had to take a degree of responsibility for their indescribable loss. By doing so, the families hoped to achieve some small measure of justice.

Dealing with an overwhelming feeling of senseless and possibly preventable loss, the grieving family members launched a legal action against Bethlehem Steel Corporation, the company they believed had betrayed and abandoned them. On January 26, 1967, almost two months to the day after the *Morrell*'s end, it was reported that the families of crew were suing Bethlehem Steel for $10 million. Twenty-eight men met their untimely death on that November night, and this money was to go to their families—the widows, children, parents, and siblings. Bethlehem Steel responded with a request that the courts limit the award to $400,000. The legal battle had begun.

An emotional and very public war of words ensued. The Coast Guard's hearings on the *Morrell* were challenged by Victor Hanson, an attorney who represented the families of sixteen crew members, as well as the Seamen's International Union. Hanson claimed that the *Morrell* hearings were biased in an effort to avoid casting blame on Bethlehem

Steel or the Coast Guard's methods of inspection. "Whitewash!" he shouted to reporters, referring to the way the Coast Guard was handling its investigation. He claimed that the Coast Guard "asked self-serving questions that were based on information supplied by the company [Bethlehem Steel], seeking to establish that the ship was in good condition. . . . If the ship was unseaworthy, there would be a question of the Coast Guard inspections."

Four years after the wreck, a settlement was finally reached between Bethlehem Steel Corporation and the families of the *Morrell*'s deceased crew. On December 7, 1970, at the U.S. District Court in Cleveland, a $2.75 million settlement was accepted by the families of the twenty-eight men. According to Hanson, it was "the largest maritime settlement in history." The judge then appointed a commissioner to determine the fairest way to distribute the lump sum among the surviving families. This process was also slow, taking more years to fully resolve.

This lawsuit against Bethlehem Steel, however, addressed only the claims filed by the families of those killed in the *Morrell* disaster. It did not include Dennis Hale, who filed his own lawsuit. Two days after his miraculous rescue and while confined to his hospital bed in Harbor Beach, Hale hired a lawyer, who filed a suit for $150,000. The lawsuit claimed that Bethlehem Steel Corporation had been negligent in its inspections, repairs, and outdated emergency equipment. In short, Hale's legal argument hinged on the premise that the *Morrell* was unsafe.

One year after the tragedy, Hale increased his claim to $500,000. By the time the other claims had been settled in December 1970, Hale's suit was all that was left. Eventually, Hale and Bethlehem Steel would reach what he termed a "fair settlement," but it was agreed that the amount would never be made public.

AN OLD SHIP'S END

The *Edward Y. Townsend* never completed her journey to Minnesota, but unlike the *Morrell*, she was able to weather the storm long enough to limp into port at Sault Ste. Marie. The huge hull fracture that she suffered in her middle marked the end of the ship's career.

The *Townsend* remained docked at the Sault for nearly two years after the great storm. The sixty-two-year-old steamer was finally sold for scrap to a salvage company in Spain. The plan was to cut up and eventually reuse the old ship's steel. On Friday the 13th, in September 1968, the *Townsend* made her unlucky departure from the Sault. Two tugboats dragged the crippled vessel eastward from Lake Superior, down Lake Huron, across Lakes Erie and Ontario, and up the St. Lawrence Seaway to the Atlantic Ocean.

But she never reached her destination. On October 7, about four hundred miles southeast of St. Johns, Newfoundland, the great freighter finally broke in two, much like her sister ship, and the tugboat crews could only watch as the once noble giant slipped peacefully to the bottom of the Atlantic.

Throughout their combined 120 years of service on the Great Lakes, the *Morrell* and *Townsend* endured and survived the most vicious storms the lakes could muster—mountainous waves, bone-chilling wind, rocky shoals, dangerous coastlines, fog, snow, ice, and torrential rains. To be sure, both ships suffered plenty of weather damage over the years. Right up to their final run, the two workhorses were always ready to be loaded with cargo for delivery to a distant port. But that unscheduled late-November departure from Buffalo steered them on a collision path with a death storm that claimed twenty-eight lives and destroyed the two sister ships.

■   ■   ■

The deadly voyage of the *Daniel J. Morrell* represents the tragic confluence of three events: a ship's struggle against the unrelenting force of wind and water on a storm-tossed lake, a young man's survival despite seemingly insurmountable odds, and Bethlehem Steel's inexplicable delay in alerting the Coast Guard about its own missing ship and crew. Together, these three events define the story of the *Morrell,* one of the most awe-inspiring, harrowing, and remarkable tales in Great Lakes maritime history.

If anything good came out of this tragedy, perhaps it was the realization that the shipping industry needed to protect sailors in every way possible. How many men had to die before ships would be built with steel that was reinforced and tested to withstand the lakes' perilous storms? How long before the crews would be provided with the survival suits and all-weather survival capsules so necessary to save their lives? And how long before the industry would recognize that the preservation of life outweighs profit? The horrific catastrophe of the *Daniel J. Morrell* served as a wake-up call for the Great Lakes shipping industry.

In the end, the great steamers continued to sail at the mercy of the lakes. Their cargoes were hauled and usually delivered on schedule. The crews still performed their duties, and though they did not speak of it, they knew that they could be just one storm away from a sudden end. Like a threatening thunderhead, the uncertainty of death loomed over the sailors and their families. And that would never change.

MORRELL CREW LIST

Arthur I. Crawley	Captain	47	Rocky River, OH
Phillip E. Kapets	First Mate	51	Ironwood, MI
Duncan R. MacLeod	Second Mate	61	Gloucester, MA
Ernest G. Marcotte	Third Mate	62	Pontiac, MI
John H. Schmidt	Chief Engineer	46	Toledo, OH
Valmour A. Marchildon	First Asst. Engineer	43	Kenmore, NY
Alfred G. Norkunas	Second Asst. Engineer	39	Superior, WI
George A. Dahl	Third Asst. Engineer	38	Duluth, MN
Norman M. Bragg	Watchman	40	Niagara Falls, NY
Stuart A. Campbell	Wheelsman	60	Marinette, WI
John J. Cleary, Jr.	Deckhand	20	Cleveland, OH
Larry G. Davis	Ordinary Deckwatch	27	Toledo, OH
Arthur S. Fargo	Fireman	52	Ashtabula, OH
Charles H. Fosbender	Wheelsman	42	St. Clair, MI
Saverio Grippi	Coalpasser	53	Ashtabula, OH
John M. Groh*	Ordinary Deckwatch	21	Erie, PA
Dennis N. Hale†	Watchman	26	Ashtabula, OH
Nicholas Homick	Second Cook	35	Hudson, PA
Chester Konieczka	Fireman	45	Hamburg, NY

David L. Price	Coalpasser	19	Cleveland, OH
Joseph A. Mahsem	Porter	59	Duluth, MN
Henry Rischmiller	Wheelsman	34	Williamsville, NY
Stanley J. Satlawa*	Steward	39	Buffalo, NY
Charles J. Sestakauskas	Porter	49	Buffalo, NY
Wilson E. Simpson	Oiler	50	Albemarle, NC
Arthur E. Stojek	Deckhand	41	Buffalo, NY
Leon R. Truman	Coalpasser	45	Toledo, OH
Albert P. Whoeme	Watchman	51	Knife River, MN
Donald E. Worcester	Oiler	38	Columbia Falls, ME

*Body never found.

† Survivor.

BIBLIOGRAPHY

BOOKS

Brown, David G. *White Hurricane: A Great Lakes November Gale and America's Deadliest Maritime Disaster.* New York: International Marine/McGraw-Hill, 2002.

Hale, Dennis; as told to Tim Juhl and Jim and Pat Stayer. *Sole Survivor: Dennis Hale's Own Story.* Lexington, MI: Out of the Blue Productions, 1996.

Hancock, Paul. *Shipwrecks of the Great Lakes.* San Diego: Thunder Bay Press, 2001.

McGreevy, Susan. "Preserving Michigan's Marine History." In *Michigan's Nautical Time Capsules.* Detroit: Dossin Great Lakes Museum, 1981, 22–26.

Parker, Jack. *Shipwrecks of Lake Huron: The Great Sweet Water Sea.* AuTrain, MI: Avery Color Studios, 1986.

Ratigan, William. *Great Lakes Shipwrecks and Survivals.* New York: Galahad Books, 1994.

Thompson, Mark L. *Graveyard of the Lakes.* Detroit: Wayne State University Press, 2000.

NEWSPAPER ARTICLES

"Aftermath of Ship Disaster." *Harbor Beach Times,* December 8, 1966, 1–2.

"Agrees to Pay $2,750,000 in *Morrell* Case." *Port Huron Times Herald,* December 9, 1970, n.p.

"Asks $200,000 in *Morrell* Suit." *Port Huron Times Herald,* January 11, 1967, n.p.

"At Least 12 Crewmen Die as Ore Ship Sinks in Lake Huron." *Los Angeles Times,* December 1, 1966, 1–3.

"'Because God Wants You to Be Alive.'" *Bay City Times,* December 1, 1966, 1–2.

"Body of Another Sailor Recovered." *Port Huron Times Herald,* December 10, 1966, n.p.

"*Bramble* May Return to Wreck Scene Wednesday." *Port Huron Times Herald,* January 17, 1967, n.p.

"*Bramble* Returns to Wreck Scene." *Port Huron Times Herald,* January 28, 1967, n.p.

"Calls for Probe into Sinking of *Daniel Morrell.*" *Huron Daily Tribune,* December 2, 1966, 1.

"Calls Probe of Sinking 'Whitewash.'" *Huron Daily Tribune,* December 6, 1966, 1.

"Captain Advised Nephews against Life of Seaman." *Huron Daily Tribune,* December 1, 1966, 10.

"Captain of Sister Ship Tells of Lake Huron Storm." *Huron Daily Tribune,* December 15, 1966, 1.

"CG to Use TV in Ship Search." *Port Huron Times Herald,* December 29, 1966, n.p.

"Cutter *Bramble* Anchored at Site of Wreck." *Port Huron Times Herald,* January 19, 1967, n.p.

"Cutter *Bramble* Plans Return to Site of Wreck." *Port Huron Times Herald,* January 21, 1967, n.p.

"Death Toll in Ship Sinking Placed at 28." *Los Angeles Times,* December 2, 1966, 4.

"Discover Wreckage Site; Harbor Beach Plans Rites." *Huron Daily Tribune,* December 5, 1966, 1.

"Divers at Scene." *Port Huron Times Herald,* December 12, 1966, n.p.

"Divers Going Down Thursday: Will Inspect *Morrell* Hulk." *Port Huron Times Herald,* January 10, 1967, n.p.

"Divers Plan to Inspect Wreck." *Port Huron Times Herald,* January 13, 1967, n.p.

"Divers Set to Look for Wreckage; Find 22nd Body." *Huron Daily Tribune,* December 12, 1966, 1.

Donahue, James. "A Man Haunted." *Port Huron Times Herald,* November 24, 1991, 1C.

———. "Hospital Nurse: 'I remember he was pleased he was alive.'" *Port Huron Times Herald,* November 28, 1986, 1A, 3A.

———. "Shipwreck Survivor Credits His Life to White-Clad Visitor." *Port Huron Times Herald,* November 24, 1991, 1C.

———. "Shipwreck Torments Survivor: 20 Years after Sinking, Horror of *Morrell* Is Still Vivid." *Port Huron Times Herald,* November 24, 1991, 1A.

———. "Stern, Bow Lay Six Miles Apart." *Port Huron Times Herald,* November 28, 1986, 1A.

———. "Survivor's Question: Why Me?" *Port Huron Times Herald,* November 24, 1991, 1A.

———. "20 Years Pass since Ship Sank." *Port Huron Times Herald,* November 28, 1986, 1A, 3A.

"Eight Crewmen Rescued at Alpena: Freighter Breaks Up in Storm." *Bay City Times,* November 30, 1966, 1, 3.

"Find Body of *Morrell* Crewman." *Harbor Beach Times,* December 15, 1966, 1.

"Find *Morrell* Crew Body." *Port Huron Times Herald,* May 27, 1967, n.p.

"Find Two Bodies from *Morrell*." *Port Huron Times Herald,* April 16, 1967, n.p.

"4 Missing *Morrell* Seamen Ruled Dead." *Port Huron Times Herald,* May 11, 1967, n.p.

"Freighter with 29 Sinks Off Thumb; One Crewman Rescued." *Port Huron Times Herald,* December 1, 1966, 1A.

Gillham, Skip. "*Daniel J. Morrell* Sank 25 Years Ago." *Port Huron Times Herald,* October 6, 1991, n.p.

―――. "Ships That Ply the Lakes." *Port Huron Times Herald,* October 30, 1977, n.p.

"Hale Tells of Ordeal on Raft." *Port Huron Times Herald,* January 19, 1967, n.p.

"Hale Testifies Ship 'Leaked Like Sieve.'" *Port Huron Times Herald,* December 24, 1966, n.p.

"Hale to Tell Story Friday." *Port Huron Times Herald,* December 22, 1966, n.p.

Harston, Earl C. "Cameras Locate Stern Section of Sunken Ship." *Port Huron Times Herald,* January 7, 1967, n.p.

"*Hobson* Skipper Testifies: Calls *Morrell* Storm One of Worst." *Port Huron Times Herald,* December 20, 1966, n.p.

"Hundred Still Searching for 17 Missing Men from Ship." *Huron Daily Tribune,* December 1, 1966, 1.

"Huron Man Asks: Why Five-Day Lag in Recovery of Body?" *Port Huron Times Herald,* December 14, 1966, 1A.

"Identifying Seaman Is Difficult." *Port Huron Times Herald,* April 16, 1967, n.p.

"Lake Huron Ship Goes Down, 12 Die: The Search for Survivors Goes On." *New York Times,* December 1, 1966, 61.

"Lakes Disaster Claims 9 Area Seamen." *Buffalo Evening News,* December 1, 1966, 1.

"Lakes Freighter Sinks; 32 Crewmen Lose Lives." *Buffalo Courier-Express,* December 1, 1966, 1.

LaLonde, Pati. "Sole Survivor Dennis Hale Was the Only Man to Survive the Wreck of the *Daniel J. Morrell.*" *Bay City Times,* November 18, 2004, n.p.

"Last Ship Victim's Body That of Wisconsin Man." *Port Huron Times Herald*, June 2, 1967, n.p.

Lewis, Ward A. "Commander of Search Plane Tells What It Is Like on Lake." *Huron Daily Tribune*, December 1, 1966, 1, 10.

"Locate Stern of *Daniel J. Morrell*." *Harbor Beach Times*, January 12, 1967, 1.

"Lone Survivor Says *Morrell* Leaked Badly." *Huron Daily Tribune*, December 27, 1966, 1.

"Lone Survivor Sues for $150,000 Damages." *Huron Daily Tribune*, December 9, 1966, 1.

"Lone Survivor Tells of Ship Sinking." *Huron Daily Tribune*, December 2, 1966, 1.

"Lone Survivor Tells of Storm." *Huron Daily Tribune*, December 20, 1966, 1.

"Lone Survivor Tells of 36 Hours on Raft." *Huron Daily Tribune*, December 1, 1966, 1.

"Lone Survivor to Testify on Wednesday." *Huron Daily Tribune*, December 13, 1966, 1.

"May 1 Deadline for Filing Claims." *Port Huron Times Herald*, January 21, 1967, n.p.

Mitchell, Jan. "Local Man Recalls Days Aboard Sunken Freighter." *Port Huron Times Herald*, December 1, 1966, 1A.

"More of Survivor's Statements Released; to Testify Friday." *Huron Daily Tribune*, December 21, 1966, 1.

"*Morrell* Built by Bay City Firm." *Bay City Times*, December 1, 1966, 1.

"*Morrell* Corrosion 'Normal.'" *Port Huron Times Herald*, March 22, 1967, n.p.

"*Morrell* Hearing Resumed." *Port Huron Times Herald*, December 14, 1966, n.p.

"*Morrell* Hunt Off, for Now: Salvage Firm Will Await Spring Thaw." *Port Huron Times Herald*, December 29, 1966, n.p.

"*Morrell* Settlement Offered." *Port Huron Times Herald*, December 8, 1970, n.p.

"*Morrell* Suit Asks $500,000." *Port Huron Times Herald,* May 19, 1967, n.p.

"*Morrell* Survivor Still Having Trouble." *Port Huron Times Herald,* March 25, 1967, n.p.

"*Morrell* Video Tapes Are Being Reviewed." *Port Huron Times Herald,* January 26, 1967, n.p.

"*Morrell* Was Seaworthy: Witness Testifies at Inquiry." *Port Huron Times Herald,* December 17, 1966, n.p.

"*Morrell* Wreck Attracts Lake Huron Divers." *Port Huron Times Herald,* November 24, 1991, n.p.

"Navy Sonar to Help in Search for Ship in Lake." *Huron Daily Tribune,* December 2, 1966, 1.

"November Gales—Bane of Great Lakes Sailors." *Bay City Times,* December 1, 1966, 8.

"Ocean Unit to Search for *Morrell.*" *Port Huron Times Herald,* January 3, 1967, n.p.

"Official Report of *Morrell* Sinking Contains New Facts." *Port Huron Times Herald,* September 15, 1967, 1A.

"One Lifeboat Never Launched." *Port Huron Times Herald,* January 23, 1967, n.p.

"1,000 Marooned by Snow: Communities Are Isolated in Michigan: Homes without Electricity." *Chicago Tribune,* November 29, 1966, 1.

"Ore Carrier Captain Testifies." *Huron Daily Tribune,* December 16, 1966, 1.

"Over 650 Attend Rites as Harbor Beach Mourns Dead." *Huron Daily Tribune,* December 7, 1966, 1.

"Owners' List of Crewmen." *Port Huron Times Herald,* December 1, 1966, 20.

Patton, Mike. "Museum Receives Piece of Sunken *Morrell.*" *Port Huron Times Herald,* August 12, 1979, 4B.

———. "'One Helicopter Landed Near a Bright Red Life Raft.'" *Port Huron Times Herald,* November 28, 1986, n.p.

———. "Tells of Air Search for Victims of Ship Tragedy. *Port Huron Times Herald,* December 1, 1966, 1A.

Patton, Mike, and Ralph Polovich. "Help Was Just 20 Miles Away." *Port Huron Times Herald,* December 2, 1966, 1A.

"Plan Probe of Lake Disaster." *Chicago Tribune,* December 2, 1966, 14.

"Recommend *Morrell* Settlement." *Port Huron Times Herald,* October 30, 1972, n.p.

"Rescue Men from Ship Near Alpena Just in Nick of Time." *Huron Daily Tribune,* November 30, 1966, 1.

"St. Clair Man on Disaster Ship." *Huron Daily Tribune,* December 1, 1966, 10.

"Says *Morrell* in Good Shape: CG Inspector Testifies." *Port Huron Times Herald,* December 21, 1966, n.p.

Schroeder, Gene. "Coast Guard Plans Inquiry." *Port Huron Times Herald,* December 2, 1966, n.p.

"Service for 28 Sailors Draws Capacity Crowd." *Port Huron Times Herald,* December 6, 1966, n.p.

"Ship-Sinking Toll 28 with 8 Missing." *Washington Post and Times Herald,* December 2, 1966, A4.

"Ship Sinks in Lake; 32 Die: Splits Apart during Gale off Michigan; One Saved, Tells Harrowing Tale." *Chicago Tribune,* December 1, 1966, 1–2.

"Ship Splits, Sinks: 28 Dead: Search Site of Tragedy for Bodies." *Bay City Times,* December 1, 1966, 1, 8.

"'Ship Spun Like Top' in Storm." *Bay City Times,* December 3, 1966, 1.

"Sister Ship of *Morrell* Doomed." *Port Huron Times Herald,* September 13, 1968, n.p.

"Sister Ship of *Morrell* Rides It Out." *Bay City Times,* December 2, 1966, 21.

Smith, Brad. "Hale's Thoughts Turn to 28 Who Died: *Morrell* Survivor Recalls Year-Ago Tragedy." *Port Huron Times Herald,* November 29, 1967, n.p.

Soini, Paul D. "Hale Tells of Ship Sinking." *Port Huron Times Herald,* December 2, 1966, 1A.

———. "Main Hull Girder Failure Blamed for *Morrell* Sinking." *Port Huron Times Herald,* August 24, 1968, 1A.

"The Sole Survivor Has Single Question: 'Why Am I Alive?'" *Buffalo Evening News,* December 1, 1966, n.p.

Solt, Bob. "Reveal Efforts Made to Contact Stricken Ship." *Port Huron Times Herald,* December 2, 1966, n.p.

———. "St. Clair Crewman's Last Letter: 'If Our Luck Holds, This Will Be Our Last Trip.'" *Port Huron Times Herald,* December 1, 1966, n.p.

"Storm Hits Eastern Lakes, South." *Chicago Tribune,* November 30, 1966, 3.

"Storm Keeps State Under Wraps: Schools Closed in Area." *Bay City Times,* November 29, 1966, 1.

"Storm Sinks Freighter, 32 Drown: 12 Bodies Found after Breakup of Big Ore Vessel." *Washington Post and Times Herald,* December 1, 1966, A1, A8.

"Storm Views in Conflict: *Ford* Skipper Says It Wasn't Unusual." *Port Huron Times Herald,* December 16, 1966, n.p.

"Storm 'Worst' He Ever Saw: *Townsend* Skipper Continues Testimony." *Port Huron Times Herald,* December 15, 1966, n.p.

"Sudden Deadly Storms a Trademark of November." *Port Huron Times Herald,* December 1, 1966, 20.

"Sunken Ship Defended by Ex-Skipper." *Port Huron Times Herald,* January 6, 1967, n.p.

"Survivor of Ship Goes Home." *Port Huron Times Herald,* December 5, 1966, n.p.

"Survivor Tells of Ordeal." *Port Huron Times Herald,* December 1, 1966, 1.

"Survivor Tells Story of Terror: Waited in Pain to Die." *Bay City Times,* 2 December 1966, 1, 5.

"Survivor to Testify." *Port Huron Times Herald,* December 23, 1966, n.p.

"Temporary Order Halts Further Suits." *Port Huron Times Herald,* January 26, 1967, n.p.

"Testifies That *Morrell* Talked with Other Ships." *Huron Daily Tribune,* December 8, 1966, 1.

"TV Lake Search for *Morrell* Under Way." *Port Huron Times Herald,* January 6, 1967, n.p.